Heaven Is Not Automatic

Make Your Adoption Sure

Heaven Is Not Automatic

Make Your Adoption Sure

April C. Pryde

© *Copyright 2018 April C. Pryde*

All rights reserved. This book is protected under the copyright laws of the United States of America. No portion of this book may be reproduced in any form, without the written permission of the publisher. Permission granted on request.

Published by: Unlock Publishing House
6715 Suitland Road
Morningside, Maryland 20746
www.unlockpublishinghouse.com
ISBN: 978-0-9991648-4-6

Unless otherwise indicated, Bible quotations are taken from:

New King James Version (NKJV): *Scripture taken from the New King James Version®. Copyright © 1982 by Thomas Nelson. Used by permission. All rights reserved.*

New International Version (NIV): *Holy Bible, New International Version®, NIV® Copyright ©1973, 1978, 1984, 2011 by Biblica, Inc.® Used by permission. All rights reserved worldwide.*

Living Bible (TLB): *The Living Bible copyright © 1971 by Tyndale House Foundation. Used by permission of Tyndale House Publishers Inc., Carol Stream, Illinois 60188. All rights reserved.*
Amplified Bible (AMP) *Copyright © 2015 by The Lockman Foundation, La Habra, CA 90631. All rights reserved.*

Amplified Bible (AMPC): Amplified Classic Edition *Copyright © 1954, 1958, 1962, 1964, 1965, 1987 by The Lockman Foundation*

The Message (MSG): *Copyright © 1993, 1994, 1995, 1996, 2000, 2001, 2002 by Eugene H. Peterson*

The Strong's Concordance App: *(Strong's Concordance is a concordance of the King James Bible (KJV) that was constructed under the direction of Dr. James Strong (1822–1894) and first published in 1890.*

Christian Bible Reference Site; *(Lockyer p. 1103)*

Printed in the United States of America January 2018

Dedication

This book is dedicated to the memory of my Mother, Frances Roberta Johnson and my Sister, Alva Frances Gibson.

When I was searching for meaning in my life, Mama told me that I needed Jesus. Not really understanding the meaning of being saved herself, I had the honor of ministering salvation to her before she went to heaven to be with Jesus. Thank you Ma, my life is forever changed.

Alva, my big sister and friend, departed this life too soon. She was one of my biggest supporters and my shopping partner. Words can't express the void I feel in my heart and in my world without her.

I also have to thank my husband Norman James "Bud" Pryde for his love, patience and overall support with this project and anything that I take on. He believes that I can do anything.

To my family, you all were my inspiration for this book. My prayer is that from this project, you will know the truth of God's Word and live for Him.

Last but not least, I want to thank my pastor, Apostle Michael A. Freeman, for supporting me in this project and writing a forward for me. I absolutely love being a partner with him and Dr. Deloris Freeman in their assignment to the Body of Christ.

Table of Contents

Dedication 7
Foreword 11
Introduction 13
The Gathering 15
Who's Welcome? (The Invitation) 28
Taking Off The Old Man And Putting On The New Man 61
So, Why Are We Here? 78
The Dangers of Not Renewing Your Mind 95
Partnering With God 120
Conclusion 124

Foreword

By Apostle Michael A. Freeman

Many write books, but few have the ability to tell life-changing stories. In this book, April tackles the taboo topic of salvation by explaining what God truly desires of us. Oftentimes there is a misconception that everyone is a "Child of God, "but in this book, April explains how to become a true Child of God.

April shares her story while infusing biblical standards and principles to help readers understand how to really live for Christ. I am so excited about this book and the impact it's sure to have on the world. It does my heart well knowing that a believer in the Body of Christ is using their gift for the glory of God.

This book not only teaches readers about receiving Jesus Christ as Lord and Savior, but also how to live a righteous lifestyle post salvation. The book address basic key principles for righteous living such as being the earth's answer and making God a priority. I look forward to the life-changing testimonies that are sure to follow.

Introduction

Heaven is Not Automatic was birthed out of my desire to fulfill the Great Commission; sharing the truth of God's Word in simplicity to those who may not otherwise read the bible. My passion is to help others understand that heaven is not a guarantee for everyone that departs this life. God loves us (His creation) so much and desires that we become His children and spend eternity with Him, but unless we understand His Kingdom (His ways of doing things), we could miss heaven. In this book, I will bring an understanding of the ways of God through His Word. I have compiled the relating scriptures that highlight the chapters presented, and I believe they will give specific truths that address this subject. The truth is, God loves us and Scripture tells us that, *"it is not His Will that any should parish" but that they come to repentance,"* (2 Peter 3:9) *because He has no pleasure in the death of the wicked.* (Ezekiel 33:11).

Some people believe that everyone will automatically go to heaven when they transition from this life. I use the word transition because when your spirit leaves your body, your spirit, who is the real you, will go on to live forever in one of two places. It's not popular nor is it acceptable to some belief systems, that God will send people to hell. The truth is, God does not send people to hell. He gives us the opportunity to choose heaven, but when we don't accept His invitation to receive Jesus, we automatically choose hell. He gives us that right. While all of us are creations of God, we are not automatically a child of God. There are requirements that have to be met before anyone can call themselves a child of God.

I pray this book gives you insight and clarity so that you might be able to make an intelligent decision and choose the Lord Jesus Christ. I desire more than anything to be obedient to the great commission. Praying with those I encounter to receive Jesus as their Lord and Savior, and disciplining them to do the same for others. As a Christian, it is my responsibility to share the Good News of the Gospel.

This book is written with scriptures compiled from the Holy Bible and my personal experiences. More than anything I want you to have the information you needed to obtain a full understanding of what salvation truly is. There may be some information that is hard for you to understand, consider the information that you can relate to, and pray for understanding for the rest. If you are reading this book and have not trusted your life to the Lordship of Jesus Christ, I pray this will be a tool that leads you to make the most important decision that you will ever make in your life and then share it with your family and friends.

John 8:32 *"And ye shall know the truth and the truth shall make you free.*

The Gathering

All around in today's society, we encounter automatic apparatuses that aide us in our daily lives. These things were designed to make life easier and safer for us in so many ways, and I have to say, I enjoy the convenience of every automatic device that I come across. When I leave my home, my first encounter with an automatic device is getting in my car. When I start my car, my seat automatically moves into the place where I've set it. I push a button, and the garage door opens. When I put my car in drive, the doors automatically lock and then all day long, I encounter automatic doors, steps, lights, faucets, toilets, paper towel dispensers, hot air dryers and the list goes on and on. And while all of these great inventions are awesome and make life easier for us, we can't adopt the automatic concept for everything, and going to heaven is one of them.

We are all familiar with the gathering. We gather more often than we care to, to celebrate the life of loved ones and friends who depart this life. It is never pleasant to say goodbye to the departed, and while this setting is a good one to address salvation, I personally used to find it difficult to engage my family and friends in a conversation about salvation. As much as I love them and know the fate of anyone who is not born-again, it was a struggle to ask them if they were spiritually prepared to meet God. The fear of rejection was very present in my life. Although it crossed my mind as I went about my life, it was an uncomfortable subject that did not have precedence over all of the other topics I talked about. I'm not proud of that. I always convinced myself that I had time to get

The Gathering

the message to them but I never knew when the unthinkable would happen.

For instance, I was not expecting or ready for the phone call I received on the morning of July 18, 2013 around 11:15 that informed me that I had just lost my sister, Alva. I remember it so vividly to this day. I was in the grocery store picking up a few items when my phone rang. I was pleasantly surprised to see that it was Alva's daughter-in-law Ebony, but when I answered the phone she was crying and sobbing, and I could not make out what she was saying or why she was crying. I said, "Ebony talk to me," but I could tell she didn't want to tell me what had happened, and I kept calling her name and asking her what was wrong. I knew it was bad, but I couldn't have imagined that it was my sister, and then she said the words, Alva was gone. WHAT DO YOU MEAN??? My mind went into a tailspin. She couldn't be dead! I just spoke with her the other day! She made plans to come to my house! I was expecting her! So many things were running through my mind in those few minutes while I was running out of the store screaming, WHAT HAPPEN TO ALVA???.. WHERE IS SHE???

In those few minutes, I knew my life would never be the same. After the initial shock of hearing that my big sister and friend was gone, I was faced with all the questions of salvation that I had not built enough courage to address with some of my family members and friends. I started fishing for the answers that I needed. Was she prepared to meet God? Will she spend eternity in heaven? Did God accept her as His? Will she greet me when I get to heaven? Did I do enough and say enough to make sure she was prepared? I was horrified at the thought of her not being ready to meet God. After I settled down from the initial shock, I gained strength from an image that I saw in my mind of one of the elders at the church praying with her at the altar. A sense of peace came over me. I knew that I had ministered to my sister on numerous occasions. I always told

The Gathering

her that she needed to have a relationship with Jesus. I know she heard me, but she didn't want to be pressured. I knew I had done my job to minister to her. I also realized in those few moments that I couldn't waste time getting the message out to others that heaven is real, but it is not automatic. At Alva's Celebration of Life Service, I looked around at all the people Alva had influenced in her lifetime and couldn't help but wonder, how many of them don't know Jesus as their Savior. So many people loved her because of her kind heart. Every Christmas she would bake the family Christmas cookies; it was a labor of love for her, and she enjoyed doing it. She was so gifted at knitting and crocheting blankets, shawls and baby clothes. She blessed so many people with her gift. I will always treasure the shawl she made for me. She also blessed us with her Popular Club business. She was a breath of fresh air to be around, and she is sorely missed.

After we said goodbye to Alva, it was no longer life as usual. I still felt the sting of feeling as if I had not said enough to encourage her to get close to Jesus. It haunted me for a while, but I had to move past that. Now, I only remember the good times we had. When we were together, I always wanted to talk about Jesus, but her words would ring in my head. "I don't want to be pressured," so I would just enjoy being with her singing old school songs as we rode around shopping and hanging out. She would always call me and say, "what cha doin"? "Come ride with me" or "Come get me if you're going anywhere." We had so much fun being together. One of my fondest memories of being with Alva was riding down Route 4, on those rolling hills that I love so much, singing the song "The Name Game." That was so much fun, and I was thanking God that I didn't get my "second" ticket on those rolling hills that day. I remember our last day together. We had a family meeting at our aunt's house, and she wanted me to pick her up because she didn't want to drive. While at the meeting, I looked at her and felt something in my spirit but I didn't know what to make of it. She looked weighed down. After the meeting, I dropped her off at home, and she asked me to come in because she wanted to show me what she'd gotten our cousin for a wedding gift, but I declined her invitation because I wanted to get home. I would have done things differently if I had known that would be the last time I would see her. Words can't express how I miss her. But now there is work to do.

Are You Prepared To Meet God?

Before I was born-again, I didn't think much about God. I thought like most people that I was ok and when I died, I would go to heaven. After all, I went to church, I prayed sometimes, and I even confessed my sins to the priest. So I thought I was good to go. But years later I found out that was not the case. I found out that I didn't know God at all and I was not prepared to meet Him. And although I didn't know Him, I later realized that in my darkest days, He was there drawing me but I just didn't know it.

My salvation journey started in Las Vegas when I called my mother and told her that something was missing in my life. Although I had a wonderful husband and a beautiful daughter, and the military life was good, I felt miserable. She told me that I needed Jesus. I remember praying and asking God, "If you're real, please help me," and guess what! He sent someone to minister to me. Denise was my neighbor in Las Vegas, who knew the Lord. She was itching to talk to me about Him. She was so bubbly and her love for the Lord was evident. It was something that I had never seen before. When she finally came over to meet me, she asked me if I was saved, and I asked her saved from what? I had no clue about salvation. I had never heard the term, "saved." When she talked about Jesus she gave me hope, and I wanted to experience what she was sharing with me. I remember one day

The Gathering

as she was talking about Jesus I asked her to hug me because I thought I could feel what she was feeling. I know that sounds crazy, but she was so full of the light of Jesus, and I was so far from the light of Jesus, but I wanted it. She planted seeds of the Word of God in my heart that I can't remember now, but I will never forget how those words made me feel. I'm a witness that the Word of God is alive. I went to church with her and gave my life to the Lord, but I didn't get a good understanding of what was taking place. I didn't continue to go to church to learn about God. I went through the motions but my lifestyle didn't change. A few months later, Denise moved away and soon after that, we moved to Myrtle Beach, South Carolina. I will pick this story up in a later chapter.

Although my mother was the one who told me I needed Jesus, she had no concept of being born-again or saved herself. She believed the same way I did, or should I say, I believed the way she did. She passed on to me what she knew about religion, but it was not the whole truth. We thought being a part of a church organization was enough, but we needed a Savior. We were accustomed to the religious rituals, and I have to admit that when I went to confession, I came out of that booth feeling free, and my conscience clear, but I still didn't know Jesus as my Savior. I had no idea that God wanted me to have a personal relationship with Him. I had no idea that I was to be a part of His redemptive plan to a dying world. As a child of God, I am challenging myself to share the love of God with those around me. God depends on me to do my part as His ambassador on earth. (2 Corinthians 5:20)

I'm spreading the "Good News" that God Loves you and your adoption into Christianity is waiting on you. Are you concerned about where you will spend eternity? Have you given it any thought? Maybe you think as I did. Perhaps you believe that you will automatically go to heaven because you are a good person. Many people believe that, but the truth is, we all need a Savior and Jesus is the only one who fits the bill. Now that I know the truth, I can't ignore the sin state of people around me and act as if I don't know the ramifications of them not knowing Jesus as their Savior. If you know for sure that you are prepared to meet God, then you should be concerned about those around you also. If you're not sure, this would be an excellent time to investigate it and be sure. At the time of yours or your loved ones death is not the time to inquire about salvation. Once you transition from this life, it's too late to do anything about it. When you transition from this life, you lose the ability to choose where you will spend eternity.

Deuteronomy 30:15 NKJV *"I have set before you life and death.... choose life".*

People believe that heaven is real, but not everyone believes that hell is real. I know people who believe in the activity of angels but don't believe in the operation of demons. The truth is, they are the same. God uses Angels; they are His messengers and they minister to the believer. Demons, on the other hand, are fallen angels being used by the devil to try to destroy believers. I wanted to share that because we believe all kinds of things that we have never investigated, and then realize somewhere down the road that we were wrong. People, in general, believe that murderers and horrible people go to hell because murder is a "real bad" sin. They categorize sin, but God does not categorize sin. They think the murderer is worse than the liar is, but to God, they are equally bad. A person that lies is just as bad as a person that murders in God's eyes because sin is sin. The Bible teaches us that *"all liars will have their place in "the lake which burns with fire and brimstones." (Revelation 21:8).* Instead of calling a lie a lie, they call it a "little white lie." Big or small, a lie is a lie, and it is deception. I apologize for going on a tangent, but that

The Gathering

example and others like it are what people use to justify their sin and make themselves feel better about the things they do. But is it worth it? Let me make myself clear, a lie will not send a born-again believer to hell because Jesus died for their past, present and future sin, but repentance will always be a requirement. Repent means to **"feel such sorrow for sin or fault as to be disposed to change one's life for the better; be penitent." It means to feel sorry; contrite for past conduct; regret or to be conscience-stricken about a past action, attitude, etc."** Repenting simply means to turn away from your sin. Once you know how God feels about any sin in your new life in Him, you will do your best to stop.

Many people don't think about God when it comes to heaven, and they just assume they are good enough to be with Him at the end of their life, as I did. Please understand, He never meant for people to end up in hell but that is where some end up because they don't accept the gift of salvation. Hell is mentioned over 100 times throughout Scripture. In Luke, Jesus Himself talked about hell and the consequences of sin. He taught about the rich man and Lazarus.

Luke 16:19-21 MSG "There once was a rich man, expensively dressed in the latest fashions, wasting his days in conspicuous consumption. A poor man named Lazarus, covered with sores, had been dumped on his doorstep. All he lived for was to get a meal from scraps off the rich man's table. His best friends were the dogs who came and licked his sores. Then he died, this poor man, and was taken up by the angels to the lap of Abraham. The rich man also died and was buried. In hell and in torment, he looked up and saw Abraham in the distance and Lazarus in his lap. He called out, 'Father Abraham, Have mercy! Send Lazarus to dip his finger in water to cool my tongue. I'm in agony in this fire.' "But Abraham said, 'Child, remember that in your lifetime you got the good things and Lazarus the bad things. It's not like that here. Here he's consoled, and you're tormented. Besides, in all these matters there is a huge chasm set between us so that no one can go from us to you even if he wanted to, nor can anyone cross over from you to us. 'The rich man said, 'Then let me ask you, Father: Send him to the house of my father where I have five brothers, so he can tell them the score and warn them so they won't end up here in this place of torment."

There is so much to this scripture, but I want to focus on the rich man. He went to hell (the place of torment), and he wanted someone to go and warn his family not to come there. We would be more inclined to believe that hell exists if someone close to us visited us from there, but that's not how it works. As a believer, I have been sent by God to tell you not to go there. I am sounding the alarm as a watchman on the wall.

Ezekiel 33:7-9 NKJV *"So you, son of man: I have made you a watchman for the house of Israel; therefore you shall hear a word from My mouth and warn them for Me. 8 When I say to the wicked, 'O wicked man, you shall surely die!' and you do not speak to warn the wicked from his way, that wicked man shall die in his iniquity; <u>but his blood I will require at your hand.</u> 9 Nevertheless if you warn the wicked to turn from his way, and he does not turn from his way, he shall die in his iniquity; but you have delivered your soul.*

Let me share with you what I received from this verse of scripture for myself. This scripture says to me that it is my responsibility to warn you so that your blood is not required on my hands. And what you must acknowledge about this scripture is that hell exists just as you acknowledge that heaven exists. God created hell for the devil and his demons. (Matthew 25:41) But those who refuse to accept Jesus as Savior will also go there.

The Gathering

2 Thessalonians 1:8-10 TLB *"bringing judgment on those who do not wish to know God and who refuse to accept his plan to save them through our Lord Jesus Christ. 9 They will be punished in everlasting hell, forever separated from the Lord, never to see the glory of his power 10 when he comes to receive praise and admiration because of all he has done for his people, his Saints. And you will be among those praising him because you have believed what we told you about him.*

This scripture might appear to be a little harsh, but these are the scriptures that are not talked about. The second half of this scripture should bring encouragement because when you accept Jesus as Savior, you will be amongst the Saints. We will talk more in-depth about salvation and accepting Jesus as your Savior in the next chapter.

I pray that this labor of love will bring awareness and reach deep down in the soul (will, mind, and emotions) of every person that reads it. God is a loving God, and He is giving you the opportunity to heed a warning if you are not born-again. Allow the scriptures to speak to you; they are not my opinion, but the Word of God. It is not too late for you to make the best decision you will ever make and then share it with your family and warn them not to go to the place of torment. What you have to understand is that Hell is real and contrary to some peoples' belief, it not going to be a party. I have heard that said before.

Matthew 13:41-43 AMP *"tells us that "The Son of Man will send out His angels, and they will gather out of His Kingdom all things that offend [those things by which people are led into sin], and all who practice evil [leading others into sin], 42 and will throw them into the furnace of fire; in that place there will be weeping [over sorrow and pain] and grinding of* *teeth [over distress and anger]. 43 Then the righteous [those who seek the will of God] will shine forth [radiating the new life] like the sun in the kingdom of their Father. He who has ears [to hear], let him hear and heed My words".*

That's another scripture that may sound scary, but please don't take it that way. These are the kinds of scriptures that must be shared because it dispels a lie, and is a warning to those who do believe that hell is a party because all of their friends are there. These scriptures will sound scary or harsh to those who don't want to change. Unfortunately, you can't pick and choose what scriptures you will believe. These scriptures are not meant to have a fire and brimstone effect. Receive it as the Father's love reaching out and telling you "not to touch the hot stove," if you will, because it's hot and it will burn you. God loves you and He gives you a free will to choose. On the other side of the coin, when you make Jesus your Savior this next scripture is a promise to you.

2 Corinthians 5:8 NKJV tells us, *"To be absent from the body is to be present with the Lord."*

When Jesus is your Savior, you go to be with Him in heaven when you leave this earth. As a believer, I am commanded to *"go out into the highways and hedges and compel them to come in, that His house may be filled." (Luke 14:23)* He wants as many as will receive Him to be a part of His family. As I stated before and contrary to popular belief, not everyone is a child of God. Here are two Scriptures that will bring the understanding of that statement.

John 1:12 NJKV *"But as many as <u>received Him</u>, to those who believe in His name: to them <u>He gave the right to become children of God</u>"*

Romans 8:14-16 NKJV *"For as many as are led by the Spirit of God, these are sons of God. For you did not receive the spirit of bondage again to fear, but you received the Spirit of <u>adoption</u> by whom we cry out, "Abba, Father." The Spirit Himself bears witness with our spirit that we are children of God,"*

These Scriptures state that those who receive Him become children of God, and those of His children that mature in Him are led by His Spirit which lives in them.

Your Adoption Is Your Choice

Ephesians 1:5 TLB *"His unchanging plan has always been to **adopt** us into his own family by sending Jesus Christ to die for us. And he did this because he wanted to"!*

Galatians 4:5-6 TLB *"To buy freedom for us who were slaves to the law so that he could **adopt** us as his very own sons. And because we are his sons, God has sent the Spirit of his Son into our hearts, so now we can rightly speak of God as our Heavenly Father."*

In these Scriptures, you see that you have to be adopted into God's family and that it's not an automatic deal just because you believe He exists. And while it is not automatic, God has made the provision for you through His Son. But you are responsible for making your adoption sure. Before I get too ahead of myself, let us look at the word salvation because it means so much more than escaping hell.

God offers you an excellent package deal. Salvation means deliverance from sin and the consequences of it, redemption or rescued. Simply put, your slate is wiped clean; God will not remember your sins. It means preservation; to preserve or deliverance from harm, ruin, or loss. It means health and to make whole. You will experience His mercy and grace. It simply means that everything you need is wrapped up in what Jesus did for you. He will take care of you if you let Him. So as you read the rest of this book, when you see the word saved and salvation take a mental note of the meaning to get the full understanding of what is being communicated to you.

God has created mankind with a place in their soul reserved for His Holy Spirit to reside in. For whatever reason, some will never get to experience their adoption and understand the real truth of their existence here on earth. This is another reason I'm writing this book. I want to join forces with the Body of Christ at large to advance the Kingdom of God and fulfill the Great Commission. It's my duty to tell people of God's great love, His provision, and also to warn them of an eternity without Jesus. Although this next scripture is primarily talking about the Christian that has gone astray, it's also applicable to the sinner that has never known God.

James 5:20 NKJV *says, "Let him know that he who turns a sinner from the error of his way will save a soul from death and cover a multitude of sins."*

I know that there are people who just do not want to hear about Jesus, I was one of those people. When I was a teenager I was not interested in being holy and set apart for God, nor did I know anything about being saved. I can remember so vividly a young man trying to witness to me on the bus. I was not interested. I realize now that he was being *"bold as a lion" (Proverbs 28:1)* and doing what all Christians are called to do. Little did I know, I was not rejecting that young man, but I was rejecting the salvation message (the adoption plan) that he was offering me. Even as a teenager, God was trying to get my

The Gathering

attention but I didn't want any part of what I thought being saved was all about. As I mentioned before, I grew up going to church, but I don't remember being taught that Jesus desired to have a relationship with me and that I needed to be born-again. If they shared it, I don't remember it. Strangely enough, Alva attended Christian school all her life and was not convinced that a relationship with Jesus was vitally necessary. That bothers me.

Let me end this chapter by saying, it's difficult to lose someone close to you, but you can find comfort when you know they were born-again and had a relationship with the Lord Jesus Christ. When you and your loved ones are born-again, you can rejoice knowing that you will see them in heaven.

Who's Welcome? (The Invitation)

There is only one word to answer that question, and that word is a resounding ... EVERYONE!

John 3:16 NKJV *"For God so loved the world that He gave His only begotten Son, that whoever believes in Him should not perish but have everlasting life."*

Whosoever is any and everyone who desires to know God. I mentioned in chapter one that it is not God's will that any should perish, but that all should come to repentance. (*2 Peter 3:9*) This chapter is power packed with many scriptures that explain how the Father loves you, and all that Jesus did to qualify you for heaven. Let us take it from the beginning. Jesus' whole purpose for leaving heaven and being born to a virgin named Mary was to redeem humanity from sin and bring us back into relationship with God.

Matthew 1:21 AMP *She will give birth to a Son, and you shall name Him Jesus (The LORD is salvation), for He will save His people from their sins."*

Acts 13:38-39 AMPC *"So let it be clearly known and understood by you, brethren, that through this Man forgiveness and removal of sins is now proclaimed to you; 39 And that through Him everyone who believes [who acknowledges Jesus as his Savior and devotes himself to Him] is absolved (cleared and freed) from every charge from which he could not be justified and freed by the Law of Moses and given right standing with God".* I love it! Your slate will be wiped clean.

1 Timothy 1:15-16 NIV *"Here is a trustworthy saying that deserves full acceptance: Christ Jesus came into the world to save sinners of whom I am the worst.16 But for that very*

Who's Welcome? (The Invitation)

reason I was shown mercy so that in me, the worst of sinners, Christ Jesus might display his immense patience as an example for those who would believe in him and receive eternal life".

Here Timothy expressed that he was the worst of sinners to encourage all other sinners that God is not interested in condemning them to hell, but that God is patient to allow anyone to come to Him and be rescued from a life of destruction. God is love, and everything that He thinks about you is from a heart of love. *"While we were still sinning, Jesus died for us." (Roman 5:8)* That says a lot about God and how He feels about you. Let's look at the Message Bible for the same scripture, starting with verse 12 because Timothy expresses why he feels this way about Jesus.

1 Timothy 1:12-16 MSG *"I'm so grateful to Christ Jesus for making me adequate to do this work. He went out on a limb, you know, in trusting me with this ministry. The only credentials I brought to it were invective and witch hunts and arrogance. But I was treated mercifully because I didn't know what I was doing didn't know Who I was doing it against! Grace mixed with faith and love poured over me and into me. And all because of Jesus. 15-16 Here's a word you can take to heart and depend on: Jesus Christ came into the world to save sinners. I'm proof, Public Sinner Number One; of someone who could never have made it apart from sheer mercy. And now he shows me off, evidence of his endless patience to those who are right on the edge of trusting him forever".*

Let's look at what Colossians has to say about what God does for those who make their adoption sure.

Colossians 1:13-14, 19-23NIV *"For He has rescued us from the dominion of darkness and brought us into the kingdom of*

Who's Welcome? (The Invitation)

the Son He loves, 14 in whom we have redemption, the forgiveness of sins. 15 The Son is the image of the invisible God, the firstborn over all creation...... 19 For God was pleased to have all His fullness dwell in Him, 20 and through Him to reconcile to Himself all things, whether things on earth or things in heaven, by making peace through His blood, shed on the cross. 21 Once you were alienated from God and were enemies in your minds because of your evil behavior. 22 But now He has reconciled you by Christ's physical body through death to present you holy in His sight, without blemish and free from accusation 23 if you continue in your faith, established and firm, and do not move from the hope held out in the gospel. This is the gospel that you heard and that has been proclaimed to every creature under heaven, and of which I, Paul, have become a servant."

God the Father put everything on Jesus, His Son, to carry out His redemptive plan. Therefore, our salvation rests on Jesus and Jesus alone. Jesus said in:

John 6:37 and 40 "All that My Father gives Me will come to Me; and the one who comes to Me I will most certainly not cast out [I will never, never reject anyone who follows Me].
Verse 40; "For this is My Father's will and purpose, that everyone who sees the Son and believes in Him [as Savior] will have eternal life, and I will raise him up [from the dead] on the last day."

Jesus understood His purpose, and He is assuring you of your place with Him. Jesus says to you (those who have received Him),

John 14:2 NKJV "In My Father's house are many mansions; if it were not so, I would have told you. I go to prepare a place for you. And if I go and prepare a place for you, I will come

Who's Welcome? (The Invitation)

again and receive you to Myself; that where I am, there you may be also."

I may not have a mansion here on earth, but Jesus has prepared one for me in heaven. Hallelujah!! If you were the only person on earth, He did it all for you. Do not go through life forfeiting all that God has for you, to include heaven because you haven't accepted His plan for your life.

My prayer is that you will be enlightened and encouraged by the scriptures you read in this book, go on to realize your purpose, and fulfill destiny. Jesus is the way and the guarantee to a fulfilled life here on earth and eternity in heaven. Jesus gives the invitation in these next two scriptures.

Matthew 11:28-30 NKJV *"Come to Me, all who labor and are heavy laden and I will give you rest. Take My yoke upon you and learn from Me, for I am gentle and lowly in heart, and you will find rest for your souls. For My yoke is easy and My burden is light".*

Revelation 3:20 NKJV *says "Behold, I stand at the door and knock. If anyone hears My voice and opens the door, I will come in to him and dine with him, and he will be with Me".*

In these scriptures, Jesus is reassuring you that everyone is welcome. You may say to yourself; I'm not burdened or overcome by anything in my life, so why do I need Jesus? As I shared a few pages back, you have to be adopted into His family. It's not an automatic deal. Jesus is our Savior and guarantee. I will continue to qualify that statement as you continue to read. Revelations 3:20 is speaking to the person that was in fellowship with God and then returned back to the world. Jesus loves you so much and is willing to receive

Who's Welcome? (The Invitation)

anyone that will come back to Him. God said He is married to the backslider (Jeremiah 3:14). I love that!!

In John Chapter 6, Jesus understands that it's His responsibility to carry out His Father's plan to everyone who says yes to His invitation. I'm personally fond of Matthew Chapter 11:28-30, and for those of you who may be burdened, Jesus already knows your condition; there is no shame in coming to Him just as are.

Here is where I pick my story back up. Before we moved to Myrtle Beach, I prayed and asked God to put people in my life that knew Him. We were starting a new chapter in our lives, as military families often do, but I knew I wanted Jesus. Well, Guess What! He did it again! My husband, Bud ended up working with Christians all around him. There were two, in particular, Yvonne and Marie, who worked directly with him, and Helen, who was the wife of a co-worker.

These three wonderful sisters would become my mentors. I guess they knew they were on an assignment because they loved on me with the Word of God and they lived it out in front of me. I remember experiencing the same feeling that I felt when my friend in Las Vegas talked to me about the Word of God. It was pure love. It was Yvonne who quoted Matthew 11:28-30 to me, and I said yes to God, again. It was music to my burdened ears because I was tired of trying to figure life out on my own. As I stated before, I was miserable. No one could see that I was struggling, but the reality is, without Jesus, there was a void in my life. I knew how to numb myself and get that temporary relief, but it never lasted. With Jesus, I no longer have to numb myself. I'm complete and free in Him because He's given me new life and everything that comes with it. After I received Jesus and understood the process of being a born-again Christian, I had the pleasure of ministering to my mother, and she received Jesus as her

Who's Welcome? (The Invitation)

Savior. Soon after she made her adoption sure, she went to be with Jesus after a battle with cancer.

Luke 19:10 NKJV tells us "For the Son of Man has come to seek and save that which was lost."

We all came into this world lost, but Jesus came to rescue us and to grant us access into an eternity in heaven with God. God has an established system in place. Once you have trusted Jesus as your Savior, He said that *"He will never leave or forsake you." (Hebrews13:5)* That's a promise you can take to the bank. Please understand that you are welcome and God desires a relationship with you. He's made all of the provision for your adoption so don't miss this great life that has been provided for you. You have the ability to make some promising things happen in your life, but going to heaven requires a Savior. Before we talk about salvation, let's explore a few scriptures that speaks to the unsaved state of a person.

The Unsaved State

No one wants to think of himself or herself as a sinner, in fact people are offended if someone addresses them in that way but that is precisely what we are when we are born into this world.

Psalms 51:5 NLT For I was born a sinner yes, from the moment my mother conceived me.

It does not get any clearer than that, but instead of being offended, let's understand how we became sinners.

Roman 3:23 NKJV tells us: "For all have sinned and fall short of the glory of God.

Who's Welcome? (The Invitation)

The problem with that is, we are not sinners because of something we've done. We inherited our sin nature from Adam, so you can blame him for your condition. Who is Adam? Adam was the first human on earth and the father of all humanity. He fellowshipped with God in the Garden of Eden, but he sinned against God when he ate the forbidden fruit. When Adam sinned against God, all of humanity fell with him. This is very good information to know and understand because no one is a sinner because of anything they've done, but the wrong immoral behavior they exhibit is because they were born with the sin nature in their DNA. I encourage you to read the entire story of Adam in Genesis 1:26, and all of chapters two and three. Let's read Romans Chapter 5,

Romans 5:12 NKJV *"Therefore, just as sin entered the world through one man,(Adam) and death through sin, in this way death spread to all men, because all sinned."*

As Romans chapter 5 continues, you'll see that God did not leave us in that condition. Although Adam's sin brought sin to all humanity, Jesus came and wiped away the sin condition of all who would receive Him, to bring us back into relationship with God.

Romans 5:14-19 GNT *"But from the time of Adam to the time of Moses, death ruled over all human beings, even over those who did not sin in the same way that Adam did when he disobeyed God's command. Adam was a figure of the one who was to come. 15 But the two are not the same because God's free gift is not like Adam's sin. It is true that many people died because of the sin of that one man. But God's grace is much greater, and so is his free gift to so many people through the grace of the one man, Jesus Christ. 16 And there is a difference between God's gift and the sin of one man. After the*

Who's Welcome? (The Invitation)

one sin, came the judgment of "Guilty"; but after so many sins comes the undeserved gift of "Not guilty!" 17 It is true that through the sin of one man death began to rule because of that one man. But how much greater is the result of what was done by the one man, Jesus Christ! All who receive God's abundant grace and are freely put right with him will rule in life through Christ. 18 So then, as the one sin condemned all people, in the same way, the one righteous act sets all people free and gives them life. 19 And just as all people were made sinners as the result of the disobedience of one man, in the same way, they will all be put right with God as the result of the obedience of the one man."

That was pretty wordy, but it doesn't get any clearer than that. What Adam did to cause us to be sinners, God reversed it when He sent Jesus. If God were ok with our sin nature, He never would have sent Jesus. It is clear that sin is not acceptable to God and Jesus is the guarantee that God used to secure your salvation and your place with Him in heaven and also to experience heaven right here on earth. So, let me not forget the most important verse of scripture; the scripture that has changed and impacted everyone's life who has read it and sincerely believes it.

Romans 10:9-10 NKJV *"that if you confess with your mouth the Lord Jesus and believe in your heart that God has raised Him from the dead, you will be saved. 10 For with the heart, one believes unto righteousness, and with the mouth, confession is made unto salvation."*

I will reiterate this point once again; God loves you and desires a relationship with you, and praying those words is where it all starts. Remember the meaning of salvation. Before Adam sinned, he fellowshipped and talked with God in the garden but when he transgressed, he was kicked out of the

Who's Welcome? (The Invitation)

garden; thus we all were kicked out; no longer in fellowship and separated from God also. Therefore, because you were born a sinner to your parents in this natural realm, you must be born-again in the spirit realm to become one of God's children. (The adoption process)

Listen to how Nicodemus preferences his question about being born-again. He was baffled about this spiritual matter and needed it explained to him. I needed it explained to me as well.

John 3:1-8 NKJV *"There was a man from the Pharisees named Nicodemus, a ruler of the Jews. This man came to Him at night and said, "Rabbi, we know that You have come from God as a teacher, for no one could perform these signs You do unless God were with him." Jesus replied, "I assure you: Unless someone is born again, he cannot see the kingdom of God." "But how can anyone be born when he is old?" Nicodemus asked Him. "Can he enter his mother's womb a second time and be born?" Jesus answered, "I assure you: Unless someone is born of water and the Spirit, he cannot enter the kingdom of God. Whatever is born of the flesh is flesh, and whatever is born of the Spirit is spirit. Do not be amazed that I told you that you must be born again. The wind blows where it pleases, and you hear its sound, but you don't know where it comes from or where it is going. So it is with everyone born of the Spirit."*

Let me explain these verses further; beginning with verse 3, when Jesus said, "Unless someone is born again, he cannot see the Kingdom of God, whatever is born of the flesh is flesh, and whatever is born of the Spirit is spirit." First of all, I want to point out that the "Kingdom of God" is not talking about heaven but the way God operates. Jesus is explaining that the physical birth and the spiritual birth are two different things.

Who's Welcome? (The Invitation)

The physical birth can be seen. We see it when babies are born in the natural, we understand it with no problem, but the spiritual birth is totally different. It cannot be seen; it's a divine encounter. Jesus associated it to the wind, which in Hebrew is the same word as spirit. We can't see the wind, but we can hear its noise and see the effects of it. Likewise, in the new birth experience, we understand its effects by the changes we see produced in the life of the one born again. It's a supernatural occurrence that takes place in the spirit of the born-again believer and will be seen outwardly over time. It is a new way of thinking, being, and living. It is amazing, but you will not understand the Kingdom of God until you have the Spirit of God living on the inside of you.

2 Corinthians 4:3 NIV *"And even if our gospel is veiled, it is veiled to those who are perishing. 4 The god of this age (devil) has blinded the minds of unbelievers so that they cannot see the light of the gospel that displays the glory of Christ, who is the image of God."*

1 Corinthians 2:14 AMP *"But the natural [unbelieving] man does not accept the things [the teachings and revelations] of the Spirit of God, for they are foolishness [absurd and illogical] to him; and he is incapable of understanding them, because they are spiritually discerned and appreciated,[and he is unqualified to judge spiritual matters]."*

The Scriptures are clear, those who are not born-again cannot understand the ways of God, but when their spiritual condition changes, from natural to spiritual or supernatural, their minds are illuminated, and they are no longer blind. It is a supernatural occurrence. It is not possible to possess the mind of God if you do not have the Spirit of God. The only way you can possess the mind of God is through a relationship with Jesus Christ and Him alone. There is no other way. You're not

Who's Welcome? (The Invitation)

saved because you've joined a church; you are saved when you are born-again. Allow me to add "born-again" alongside "saved and salvation" because all three mean the same thing. This scripture bears repeating:

Acts 4:12 NKJV *"Nor is there salvation in any other, for there is no other name under heaven given among men by which we must be saved."*

You might ask, "How can someone change from their old way of thinking?" It is possible, and I'm a living witness of that truth. I did not understand it all at once, but as I spent time in the presence of God and going to church to hear the Bible taught, I began to put off my old way of thinking. It was becoming easy to change because my DNA had changed. I was now washed in the Blood of Jesus and shared His DNA.

Ephesians 2:13 AMP *But now [at this very moment] in Christ Jesus you who once were [so very] far away [from God] have been brought near by the blood of Christ.*

Are You A Saint?

In conversation, have you ever heard someone say of someone they know, "He's a Saint or she's a Saint"? What do they mean by that? Are they really a Saints or do they see character traits that perhaps they don't see on most people? I've heard that said about people that I know are good people, but they were not a Saint because Jesus was not their Lord and Savior. So, why do people say that? They are referring to a person that displays character traits of what they think a "Saint" would have. We all know that person; they are the soft-spoken person who will go out of their way to take care of you. Their name will

Who's Welcome? (The Invitation)

always be associated with good things. They are pillars in their communities and so on, but are they "Saints"? Without being aware of the verse in scripture that tells us *"all have sinned and come short of the glory of God," (Romans 3:23)* we put them up on a pedestal. It is out of innocence or ignorance that we do that because we want to give people their props (due respect) when we see character traits that are outside of our norm. Most people do not carry themselves in the unique way as to be characterized as saintly, but let's be clear on what a Saint is. A Saint is someone who has said yes to the established redemptive plan of God by making Jesus their Savior and has dedicated their life to the work of the kingdom. They understand that God has a bigger plan for their lives. They discover what that plan entails and begin on their journey to accomplish it. They die to themselves and live for God. And having said that, I want to express that Saints do get to have fun and realize their dreams as well. They put God's desires first and allow God to also be involved in their personal desires.

Psalms 37:4 NKJV commands us to *"Delight yourself in the Lord, and He shall give you the desires of your heart."*

When we delight to do the Father's will, He is delighted to give us our desires. That is a promise that we can stand on. You cannot be caught up with what a person looks like or the character traits they display. What does God say about a person and how does He rate their life? We can be misled by looking at the outward appearance and behavior of people even if they display a kind and gentle lifestyle. For instance, let's look at the Amish community. They are called the "Gentle People" and that they are. They live a simple lifestyle by giving up life's modern conveniences based on their interpretation of what they read in the Bible without Holy Spirit leading them. They believe that if they abstain from modern worldly conveniences, they are close to God. They have based their salvation on their own goodness by what they do and don't do, and not on what God did in the death, burial, and resurrection of Jesus Christ. How does God rate that? Just because one appears "saintly" on the outside does not mean that they meet His standard in their heart. It is not based on their own goodness. That behavior is called self-righteousness, which is a form of legalism because they are good at following the "do's and don'ts of the law (The Old Testament). Anyone operating in self-righteousness is saying that they can generate righteousness all by themselves without Jesus, and they will be accepted by God. That's just not true. In His day, Jesus dealt harshly with the Pharisees about their self-righteous actions. Read the account of the Pharisee and the tax collector in Luke 18:9-14.

Matthew 23:27 AMP *"Woe to you, [self-righteous] scribes and Pharisees, hypocrites! For you are like whitewashed tombs which look beautiful on the outside, but inside are full of dead men's bones and everything unclean."*

The Jews were also guilty of self-righteousness, but Paul dealt with them. (Romans 2). Jesus also had to inform His disciples that "without Me you can do nothing." (John 15:5)
I think we all have a tendency to go there, but we have to understand that all of our righteousness is offensive to God.

Isaiah 64:6 AMPC tells us that *"all of our righteousness (our best deeds of rightness and justice) is like filthy rags or a polluted garment."*

Our righteousness must come through Jesus. I learned this information about the Amish, from a friend, whose family converted to Christianity from the Amish community when her dad read in scripture that they must be born-again, at

Who's Welcome? (The Invitation)

which time they converted to Christianity and left the Amish community. Although they left the Amish community, they are still very conservative, but the point is this, they are saved and ready to meet God because they are born-again and not because they avoid the world.

Jesus sends us out into the world to reconcile man back to God. I mentioned that, but I will talk more about that in another chapter. You have to be careful that you are not doing what the scripture warns you not to do. If you are comparing yourself to people that are doing what "sinners" do, it may give you a sense of being good or better. The Word tells us *"man looks at the outward appearance, but God looks at the heart." (1 Samuel 16:7)*

Here is another example that I will share. You may see someone who looks like a real tough guy, but that person could be a mover and shaker in the Kingdom of God. Saints today have blue, purple, and pink hair and they love God with all their hearts. They have tattoos all over their bodies, but they are making an impact in the kingdom because of the revelation they received when they made Jesus Lord. I remember seeing a pack of Harley Davidsons going down the road representing Jesus as their Lord and Savior. They had on their bandannas, leather, and tattoos everywhere. They didn't appear to be Saints on the outside but on the inside, they met the requirement by being filled with the love of Jesus. Just by riding down the street, they were witnessing to the world that Jesus is their Savior. That spoke volumes to those who saw them. They were not keeping it to themselves, but they went out to the highways and byways to compel others to come into the Kingdom.

2 Corinthians 10:12 NKJV tells us that *"when they measure themselves with themselves and compare themselves with one another, they are without understanding and behave unwisely."*

Who's Welcome? (The Invitation)

Jesus Christ is the only one that you are to compare yourself to; He is our Holy example. However, there is nothing wrong with looking up to someone who is mentoring you in your Christian walk but they should be following Christ.
(1 Corinthians 11:1)

We are still talking about saints so let me share this scripture.

*The second half of **Romans 8:9** says: Now, if any man does not have the Spirit of Christ, he is not His.*

That scripture speaks for itself and cannot be misunderstood. Unfortunately, not everyone knows that scripture. People believe that all people are God's people, but the Bible says otherwise. If you do not have the Spirit of God living on the inside of you, you are not a Saint, in others words, not His. We have all heard it said, "We are all God's children" but that is not true. What qualifies you to become His child is receiving Jesus and possessing His Spirit on the inside. Read what Jesus said to the scribes and Pharisees.

John 8:42-44 NKJV *"Jesus said to them, 'If God were your Father, you would love Me, for I proceeded forth and came from God; nor have I come of Myself, but He sent Me. 43 Why do you not understand My speech? Because you are not able to listen to My word. 44* ***You are of your father the devil*** *and the desires of your father you want to do. He was a murderer from the beginning and does not stand in the truth because there is no truth in him. When he speaks a lie, he speaks from his own resources, for he is a liar and the father of it."*

I shared this scripture only to show you that not everyone is a child of God. Some are of their father, the devil. It is God's desire that all people would come to Him in repentance and

Who's Welcome? (The Invitation)

become His child but not everyone will. So once again, when we come across the word "Saint" in the scriptures, it is referring to those who have received Jesus as their Savior and Lord. They are set apart ones; they have dedicated themselves to God to bring about restoration in the lives of those around them. They understand that they have been created for a higher purpose than what they desire in life for themselves. When a believer transforms his/her mind from the old natural way of thinking and washes their minds with the Word of God, their minds will be renewed and their behavior will become more and more Christ-like. There will be a noticeable difference in their walk, talk, and overall behavior. One of my favorite things to witness is the renewed mind of someone that I knew before they were saved, living by the world's standards, now displaying a lifestyle in God. When I witness that, I know that only God can transform a person in that manner. I am very skeptical when I see someone who says they are born-again but they never change. If I can't see a noticeable difference in a person's lifestyle, I question if they have had a genuine born-again experience with the Lord Jesus Christ. They may still struggle with some things in their lives, and that is ok with God, but their overall countenance and life will change. I am not judging them, but I am looking for the fruit of the Spirit to manifest in their life. There are people that have not accepted Jesus as Lord and Savior, and that is ok if they do not want to go to heaven. God will never make a person accept Him. He gives us the freedom to choose. He does leave that decision up to the individual, but scripture tells us;

Deuteronomy 30:19 NKJV *"I call heaven and earth as witnesses today against you, that I have set before you life and death, blessing and cursing; therefore choose life, that both you and your descendants may live;"*

Who's Welcome? (The Invitation)

Choosing Jesus is choosing life for you and your family because if you're born-again, it's likely that your household will be also. God gives us the choice. But there are people who feel that depending on God is a sign of weakness and that He is a crutch for those who cannot handle life on their own. They do not need God because they are making it in life on their own.

But **Matthew 16:26-27 NKJV** says, *"For what profit is it to a man if he gains the whole world and loses his own soul? Or what will a man give in exchange for his soul?"*

No doubt, people can make a good life for themselves and their families; they do it every day. But you must understand that your career is not your main purpose for being on this earth, unless it is advancing the kingdom. When you discover your kingdom purpose, if you haven't already, offer it to God. He wants to be a part of it all. He paid a great price to guarantee your place in His Kingdom. Why would you choose to live without Jesus when He was sent to redeem you from a life of destruction that you innocently inherited? If you are prosperous in every area of life without Jesus, you lack the most important thing, and that is a relationship with the One who blessed you with the means to get everything you have.

Deuteronomy 8:18 NKJV *And you shall remember the L__ORD__ your God, for it is He who gives you power to get wealth, that He may <u>establish His covenant</u> which He swore to your fathers, as it is this day.*

It reminds me of the parable of the rich young ruler.

Luke 12:16-21 MSG; *"Then He told them this story; 'The farm of a certain rich man produced a terrific crop. He talked to himself: What can I do? I'll tear down my barns and build*

Who's Welcome? (The Invitation)

bigger ones. Then I'll gather in all my grain and goods, and I'll say to myself, Self, you've done well! You've got it made and can now retire. Take it easy and have the time of your life!' Just then God showed up and said, 'Fool! Tonight you die. And your barn full of goods - who gets it?' That's what happens when you fill your barn with Self and not with God".

Success can't guarantee you a place in heaven, but a plan of salvation is freely offered to anyone who will receive it.

Salvation Is Explained

Salvation is offered through a relationship with The Lord Jesus Christ. Jesus came to seek and save the lost, as previously stated. There are no ifs, ands, or buts about it, Jesus is the Savior of the world. So what do you say to people who believe that there are other avenues into heaven? I have heard it said that Jesus could not be the only way to heaven. Jesus said in:

John 14:6 NKJV *"I am the way, the truth, and the life, no man can come to the Father except through me."*

Acts 4:12 MSG *"Salvation comes no other way; no other name has been or will be given to us by which we can be saved, only this one."*

2 Corinthians 5:21 NKJV *"For He made Him who knew no sin to be sin for us, that we might become the righteousness of God in Him."*

2 Corinthians 5:21 MSG *"How? you ask. In Christ. God put the wrong on him who never did anything wrong, so we could be put right with God."*

Who's Welcome? (The Invitation)

I can give you a lot of commentary on these scriptures, but I don't think it's necessary. No one can argue with the Word of God. God gave Jesus the where-with-all to carry out the entire plan of salvation, being the only sacrifice to carry out the death, burial and resurrection. Jesus' shed blood on Calvary cleanses the unbeliever and frees them from the destruction of sin. As I said before, Jesus and Jesus alone, is the mediator between sinful man and a Holy God.

Hebrews 12:24 a AMPC "And to Jesus, the Mediator (Go-between, Agent) of a new covenant,"

He has also gone and prepared a place in heaven for those who will receive His invitation.

John 14:2 NKJV *"In My Father's house are many mansions; if it were not so, I would have told you. I go to prepare a place for you. And if I go and prepare a place for you, I will come again and receive you to Myself; that where I am, there you may be also."*

As for me, I'm going all the way with Jesus. I will look to Him for the rest of my life because He is the *"Author and Finisher of my faith."(Hebrews 12:2)*. When Jesus stated that, "it is finished" on the cross, the fate of the believer was sealed. God has sealed the believer and *"given us His Spirit in our hearts as a guarantee."(2 Corinthians 1:22)* So now that you have learned that Jesus is the only way to heaven let's talk about the process of renewing your mind.

Renewing Your Mind

What is renewing your mind? People who don't understand spiritual transformation call this "brainwashing." I have heard people say things like, "they are brainwashing people in that church." Well if it's a good Bible teaching church and they're teaching the unadulterated truth of the Word of God, that is exactly what's supposed to happen. The biblical term for that is called "Renewing the Mind."

Romans 12:2 NKJV *"And do not be conformed to this world, but be transformed by the renewing of your mind, that you may prove what is that good and acceptable and perfect will of God."*

Ephesians 4:23 NKJV *"and be renewed in the spirit of your mind,"*

That's exactly what I did. I spent time with God in prayer and read the Bible. I grew as a Christian becoming familiar with who I am in God, and what He expects of me as His child. When I began to experience God in ways I didn't know were possible, my focus changed, and I started to seek Him all the more. I was just like a child again looking to my Heavenly Father for everything that I needed. To my amazement, He wanted me to cast all of my cares and worries to Him, and He would take care of me.

1 Peter 2:2 AMP *"Like newborn babies you should crave (thirst for, earnestly desire) the pure (unadulterated) spiritual milk, that by it you may be nurtured and grow unto [completed] salvation,"*

Who's Welcome? (The Invitation)

It didn't matter to Jesus how my life started out, and where I came from. When the Good News was presented to me, I embraced it, and now I am a citizen of heaven.

Philippians 3:20 AMP *But [we are different, because] our citizenship is in heaven. And from there we eagerly await [the coming of] the Savior, the Lord Jesus Christ;*

I enjoy the idea of my citizenship being in heaven. I also realize that being a citizen of heaven is a responsibility not to be taken lightly. It will be an on-going process of renewing my mind to that fact. It will be an on-going process but one I will never regret growing through. I understand that I must abide with Him to bear the fruit that I want to represent Him properly.

John 15:4 NKJV *"Abide in Me, and I in you. As the branch cannot bear fruit of itself, unless it abides in the vine, neither can you, unless you abide in Me."*

Making Jesus Lord

Making Jesus Lord is unfortunately where some people stop growing. They will accept Him as Savior so that they will not go to hell (fire insurance) but they don't submit to His Lordship. Making Jesus Lord is all about submission. To submit is to yield to the control and will of another and in this case, it's Jesus. When you become a Christian you start the process of denying yourself, and once again, this is done by renewing your mind. You will notice that theme throughout this book. Renewing my mind was easier in some areas of my life than others. It was a total mind shift from how I used to operate in my former lifestyle, but because I came to God out of desperation, what did I have to lose? Doing life my way

Who's Welcome? (The Invitation)

wasn't working so why would I continue doing my own thing? I submitted myself to the instructions that I learned when I went to church and as I spent time reading the Bible and praying. Reading and praying is another theme you will read throughout this book. I grew in my new lifestyle, allowing Jesus to be Lord in my life. While I'm explaining this, I feel compelled to say that God is a loving God. He is kind and merciful and gives us the space to grow, so don't be overwhelmed with this information. It's all about developing a relationship with Him. Now, having said that, as you grow, you will begin to notice convictions about some of your behaviors and favorite pastimes that were not an issue before. I would encourage you to pay attention to that. Let me give you an example of what I'm talking about. Before I was a believer, cursing and fowl language came natural to me. It was a part of my natural DNA, but after my conversion, I was very uncomfortable using bad language. I submitted to that conviction and stopped. I simply yielded to what I knew God wanted. God is Holy and He desires for His Children to be holy. What does being holy mean? Before I was born again, when I heard the word holy, I thought I had to stop wearing pants, makeup, jewelry, and look unattractive. I thought I had to wear pantyhose and dresses all the time. As a teenager, I couldn't embrace that idea. But let's look at what holy means. **It means "dedicated or devoted to the service of God; saintly, godly; pious; devoted: a holy life; have a spiritual pure quality.** As I began to be exposed to different Christian denominations, I saw that they loved God with all their hearts and they were comfortable doing it. They were wearing pants, makeup and jewelry. Hallelujah!! We should be conservative in what we wear as not to expose ourselves in an inappropriate way causing our brothers and sister to stumble. We can be devoted to God and living a pure life in casual clothing. But you must allow Jesus to take you from your old way of living to the new way of living in Him. All activities are not suitable

Who's Welcome? (The Invitation)

for the Born Again Believer. Let's talk about sanctification. The sanctification process is vital in your walk with God; it's in line with "Making Jesus Lord". Sanctification means being set apart for God's purpose. In establishing any special relationship, it's going to take quality time getting to know each other. We need that time with God in prayer and reading His Word because a healthy relationship is not possible without spending quality time. In spending time with God, you learn things about Him that only He can reveal to you. Throughout this book, I share some of my special moments and testimonies to help you understand how He operates, but He wants you to have your own special moments. Please don't stop at Salvation, there is so much more waiting for you. Give Him access to every area of your life and He will perfect you. Allow Him to be the driver of your life. I'm reminded of the lyrics to the song "Jesus Take The Wheel". It says,

"Jesus take the wheel, take it from my hands 'cause I can't do this on my own, I'm letting go, so give me one more chance and save me from this road I'm on, Jesus take the wheel". Courtesy of AZLyrics.

Let's read what Jesus said to His disciples.

Matthew 16:24-25 *Then Jesus said to his disciples, "Whoever wants to be my disciple must deny themselves and take up their cross and follow me. For whoever wants to save their life will lose it, but whoever loses their life for me will find it.*

Read the same verse in the Message Bible.

Matthew 16:24-26 MSG *Then Jesus went to work on his disciples. "Anyone who intends to come with Me has to let Me lead. You're not in the driver's seat; I am. Don't run from suffering; embrace it. Follow Me, and I'll, show you how.*

Who's Welcome? (The Invitation)

Self-help is no help at all. Self-sacrifice is the way, my way, to finding yourself, your true self. What kind of deal is it to get everything you want but lose yourself? What could you ever trade your soul for?"

When you receive Jesus as Savior, submit to His Lordship also. Don't short change yourself. Get all that God has for you. Making Jesus Lord, will guarantee you a fulfilled and successful Christian journey. Be faithful to Him as He is faithful to you. There is much that God wants to do in and through your life, as we will explore later on.

My born again experience was nothing short of miraculous. I felt the weight of the world lifted off of me and I knew in my heart that I was different. I could not explain it but my world had changed, and it had changed for the better. Every day I experienced God, and it was fresh and new. But I didn't stop there. I desired the Word of God before I knew that's what the Bible instructed me to do. I desperately wanted to know how to live for God and I have never turned back. As a babe in Christ, He treated me just like a good loving parent treats their new infant. He pampered me for months as I grew. Any question I asked, the answer came immediately; I would open the Bible and the answer would be right there. He was blowing my mind. But then I had to learn how to walk this new way, and the more I grew in God, the more I learned to trust His Spirit to navigate me without needing someone in the natural to hold my hand. I wanted to please God, so I practiced His presence. Practicing His presence means that I was fully aware that He was with me. I didn't want to do anything that would jeopardize my new found freedom in Him. My home became a place where the Spirit of God and angels resided. I was often told that my home was a solace to those who visited me. It was not always that way. I'm not perfect, and I do miss the mark as I continue to grow, but it's nowhere what it used to

Who's Welcome? (The Invitation)

be. I can't believe that there was ever a time that I didn't want salvation, (deliverance, provision, health, preservation, victory), especially now that I know what the word "salvation" means. I want to be used of God. In retrospect, another reason I didn't want God was because I thought I couldn't have fun anymore. I now realize I believed a lie. The truth is, I am happier now and have joy that is not based on any particular activity that I think I must engage in. There is nothing that compares to my new life in Christ and being in fellowship with an All Powerful, All Knowing, and Ever Present God, who desires to use me for His glory. That's Awesome to me!!!
I have come to understand that we're not truly free until we don't need vices to make us happy. Vice means an immoral or evil habit or practice. We must understand that freedom is not needing the vices and still experiencing joy and gladness in our souls that comes as a result of just knowing Jesus. People want to be free to do the things they want to do, but you have to investigate what's driving that desire. When you become a born again Christian, you have to look carefully at your desires and behavior. Are they coming from your old nature or new nature? I want to encourage you that whatever you give up to serve the Lord Jesus is nothing compared to how He wants to bless you. I promise you that you will not miss your old life when you submit entirely to the Lord.

1 Corinthians 2:9 NKJV *tells us "Eye has not seen, nor ear heard, nor have entered into the heart of man the things which God has prepared for those who love Him."*

It's scriptures like this one that makes me want to live for God and see all that He has for me, but more importantly, I don't want to play with my salvation. Making Jesus Lord is not grievous. He will transform you and enhance everything about your life for the good. If you don't know the Lord Jesus Christ as your personal Lord and Savior, praying the prayer of

Who's Welcome? (The Invitation)

salvation will be the most important prayer you will ever pray in your life. *"Jesus is the way the truth and the life, no man can come to the Father except through Him." (John 14:6)*

If you are ready to pray this prayer, I would ask that you settle yourself, and with a contrite heart pray this prayer with all sincerity. Anyone can utter words but I want it to be a conscious decision on your part to realize what is happening to for you as you pray. This prayer is for the unbeliever and the backslider. As I shared earlier, God is married to the backslider and will always receive them back (Jeremiah 3:14). Pray this prayer with a heart of expectation, and get up knowing that you are a new creation in Christ. Pray this prayer!

Prayer of Salvation: Heavenly Father, Your word says, the one who comes to You, You will not turn away. I come to You repenting of my sins. I invite Jesus to come into my heart and be my Lord and Savior. Thank you Father for receiving me as your child. I am a new creature in Christ and Heaven is now my home, in Jesus name. Amen!!

I pray that you have made your adoption sure. If you have prayed that prayer, the Spirit of the Lord has moved in and has taken up residency in your spirit; that part of you that was empty before He came in.
Congratulations are in order! The angels in heaven are celebrating in your honor.

Luke 15:10 NKJV *"Likewise, I say unto you, there is joy in the presence of the angels of God over one sinner that repents."*

You are born-again (saved) and heaven is now your home. Through the shed Blood of Jesus, your slate has been wiped

Who's Welcome? (The Invitation)

clean, and God does not remember your sin. Your sanctification process is in progress. Now, when God sees you, He sees you through the shed blood of Jesus Christ. You have been acquitted and justified (just as if you had never sinned). You don't have to feel any guilt or condemnation about your past.

2 Corinthians 5:17 NKJV *Therefore, if anyone is in Christ, he is a new creation; old things have passed away; behold, all things have become new.*

God is now your Heavenly Father. Jesus is your Big Brother, your Savior, your Lord, and Holy Spirit is on standby to assist you in your new life. I pray that you will have an awareness of God's love for you; that He is a loving Father who is ready to show you how great you are in Him. In the future, when you sin, remember this next scripture.

1 John 1:9 NKJV *If we confess our sins, He is faithful and just to forgive us our sins and to cleanse us from all unrighteousness.*

We are human and will sin, but He is faithful to forgive you. Before we go any farther, tell someone about the most important decision that you just made. Confirm your decision by sharing with someone that you have changed the course of your life. Don't be a closet Christian who's ashamed of your new life in Christ, share the good news. He's not ashamed to be associated with you, so don't be ashamed of Him.

Mark 8:38 TLB *"And anyone who is ashamed of me and my message in these days of unbelief and sin, I, the Messiah, will be ashamed of him when I return in the glory of my Father, with the holy angels."*

Who's Welcome? (The Invitation)

Palms 107:2 NKJV *"Let the redeemed of the LORD say so, Whom He has redeemed from the hand of the enemy,"*

You have been redeemed from a life of destruction, and free to live for Jesus.

Now, I have some exciting news for you. To the one who has made your adoption sure, you are an **Heir** of God. An heir is someone who inherits or is entitled to inherit the rank, title, position, etc., of another. Throughout the Bible, scripture confirms your status.

Roman 8:16-17 NKJV *The Spirit Himself bears witness with our spirit that we are children of God, [17] and if children, then* **heirs—heirs** *of God and joint heirs with Christ, if indeed we suffer with Him, that we may also be glorified together.*

Titus 3:6-7 NKJV *whom He poured out on us abundantly through Jesus Christ our Savior, [7] that having been justified by His grace we should become* **heirs** *according to the hope of eternal life.*

Galatians 3:29 NKJV *And if you are Christ's, then you are Abraham's seed, and* **heirs** *according to the promise*

Hebrews 6:13-14, 17-19 *For when God made the promise to Abraham, He swore [an oath] by Himself, since He had no one greater by whom to swear, [14] saying, "I WILL SURELY BLESS YOU AND I WILL SURELY MULTIPLY YOU......[17] In the same way God, in His desire to show to the* **heirs** *of the promise the unchangeable nature of His purpose, intervened and guaranteed it with an oath, [18] so that by two unchangeable things [His promise and His oath] in which it is impossible for God to lie, we who have fled [to Him] for refuge would have strong encouragement and indwelling strength to hold tightly* to the hope set before us. *¹⁹ This hope [this confident assurance] we have as an anchor of the soul [it cannot slip and it cannot break down under whatever pressure bears upon it]*

I wanted to share the last two scriptures together to show you that, in the same way God made promises to Abraham, He now makes the same promises to you. He swore an oath that He will surely bless us. He wants us to be convinced beyond any doubt that by His promise and His oath, He is here for us in any way that we need Him. Verse 16 explains that men swear on an oath by one greater than themselves, but God swore by Himself because there is no one greater than He is. Because the oath serves as confirmation of what has been said, it should end all of the disputes about any concerns we have as God's **heirs**. He wants us to settle that promise in our hearts, and wants this hope; confident assurance, to be the anchor of our souls. We know the function of an anchor; it keeps a boat from drifting away from where it is fastened. Keep these words on the forefront of your mind and don't doubt God's love for you. What do you need from your Heavenly Father? His promises are endless. I hope that encouraged you to continue on in your relationship with God.

Now it's time to learn how to grow in your new life. I want to remind you that your new life in Christ started with a confession of faith. You had to *"confess with your mouth and believe with your heart"* that you were saved. With those same actions (confessing & believing), you will build your new life in Christ. In fact,

Hebrews 4:14 NIV instructs us to *"hold firmly to the faith we profess."*

Who's Welcome? (The Invitation)

God spoke the universe into existence, and He made us speaking spirits also. God said "*Let there be*"; and it was. I submit to you; we will create our reality also by speaking the Word over our lives. Your confession is your profession. That simply means that you will practice speaking the Word of God over your life. You must say what God says about you and believe by faith that He can bring it to pass in your life. Let me bring more clarity to what I am saying. When you are sick in your body, instead of confessing that "I am sick"; confess "by His stripes I am healed" because that is what we are instructed to do. When we do this, we are not denying that we feel bad. The **fact** is, we are sick, BUT the **truth** is, by His stripes we were healed (1 Peter 2:24). Our focus should always be on the truth of God's Word. That is not name it and claim it, that's the language of the believer. To make sure you understand what I'm saying, here is another example. You may have committed a crime, but what you did is not who you are as a redeemed child of God. Remember that your slate has been wiped clean and you can meditate on what God has called you. There are programs that will have us confess our faults or dysfunction before a group to acknowledge that we are damaged. And while we must acknowledge the issue before healing can begin, instead of confessing the issue, we confess God's Word over our new and reformed lives. So when the enemy whispers to you that you are a murder, a thief, or whatever the issue is, you can say to him, "I have been redeemed and God loves me". The Bible teaches us that we have what we say, so I say to you to confess what you want to see. This new way of doing things does not have to take long. The time you devote to your new life, is how fast you will grow in the process. The important thing is that you are on your way to a new and exciting way of life. Find comfort in your new position in Christ; hold firmly to what you are learning.

Proverbs 18:21 NKJV *"Death and life are in the power of the tongue."*

We will talk more about faith and what it means in your walk with Christ. The chapters following will assist you in understanding the process.

Prayer- Communication With God

Prayer is a dialog between us and our Heavenly Father. It is how we will fellowship with Him. Prayer should be the foundation of all the endeavors we take on because we are instructed to *"Trust in the LORD with all your heart and lean not unto your own understanding. In all thy ways acknowledge Him, and He shall direct your paths"*. (Proverbs 3:5-*6)*

Trusting God is necessary for developing our relationship with Him. We want Him to direct our path because He will not steer you wrong. Familiarizing yourselves with His Word (Bible) is vital because in prayer you practice confessing His Word and believing it in your heart. When you are praying about a situation, never look at it from a hopeless standpoint, instead purpose to see it from God's perspective. He is greater than our situations and He is already in our future, now. His perspective of any situation is always better than ours. When we get God involved in our situations, we come out on top. Our Heavenly Father is a promise keeper; if He said it in His Word, He can bring it to pass in your life.

Jeremiah 1:12 AMP tells us that *"for I am [actively] watching over My word to fulfill it."*

Hebrews 4:12 AMP tells us that *"For the Word of God is living and active and full of power [making it operative,*

Who's Welcome? (The Invitation)

energizing, and effective]. It is sharper than any two-edged sword, penetrating as far as the division of the soul and spirit [the completeness of a person], and of both joints and marrow [the deepest parts of our nature], exposing and judging the very thoughts and intentions of the heart.

The Word of God is powerful, and in prayer is where you will exercise the Word over all your situations, knowing with confidence that God is taking care of it. We have to understand that He is behind the scene orchestrating our lives and working it for our good. We want to take the "Sword of the Spirit" (The Word) in prayer always. Read Ephesians 6 in its entirety.

Ephesians 6:17-18 NKJV *"And take the helmet of salvation, and the sword of the Spirit, which is the word of God: 18 Praying always with all prayer and supplication in the Spirit, and watching thereunto with all perseverance and supplication for all saints;*

God watches over His Word to bring it to pass in our lives. It can't get any better than that. He instructs us on what to do and if we want His results, we must submit to what He says. The choice is ours. He commands us to "Pray without ceasing." *(1 Thessalonians 5:17)* We have to pray because this is how we Get God on the scene when we need Him. Praying without ceasing doesn't mean we stay on our knees praying all day, but we can stay in a posture of prayer in our hearts for all types of prayer needs.

2 Chronicles 7:14 NIV says, *"If my people, who are called by my name, will humble themselves and pray and seek my face and turn from their wicked ways, then I will hear from heaven, and I will forgive their sin and will heal their land."*

Who's Welcome? (The Invitation)

We are God's people and He wants us to pray so that He can not only heal the land, but He also wants to heal whatever is not well in our lives. Whether it is our bodies, marriage, finances or any other situations. There are promises in the Word that will address every need that we will ever have. We simply have to be obedient in studying the Word of God and be consistent in prayer, so when we are faced with a problem, we can say as Jesus said; "It is written," and then, stand on the Word of God. Also, we are instructed to pray in Jesus' name.

John 16:23 NKJV *"Most assuredly, I say to you, whatever you ask the Father in My name He will give you."*

Mark 11:24 NIV *"Therefore I tell you, whatever you ask for in prayer, believe that you have received it, and it will be yours."*

1 John 5:14-15 NIV *"This is the confidence we have in approaching God: that if we ask anything according to his will, (His Word) he hears us. And if we know that He hears us whatever we ask we know that we have what we asked of him."*

God's promises are to the believers so we can be confident that He is there for us.

Hebrews 4:12-16 *"Let us therefore come boldly to the throne of grace that we may obtain mercy and find grace to help in time of need."*

Not everyone has that privilege. I wanted to share these prayer scriptures to give you some insight into how important prayer is in the life of the believer, but this is by no means all there is to prayer.

Taking Off The Old Man And Putting On The New Man

Introducing Holy Spirit

Before we talk about taking off the old man and putting on the new man, I want to introduce you to Holy Spirit, the One who will give you the **power** (ability) to accomplish this process. Let me explain further. When we asked Jesus to come into our lives to be our Savior, The presence of His Spirit did just that. He came in and gave us everything that pertains to life and godliness, according to *(2 Peter 1:3)*. He made us righteous. He is the guarantee of our salvation. He took all of our bad and gave us all of His goodness. All of the sin we committed was all wiped away, and we are free from it. I call it "The Great Exchange." That might sound too good to be true, but that is what happens, and we believe it by faith. But we can't stop there. Scripture teaches us that we need power. This power comes when we pray for the gift that Jesus promised His disciples. We call this process being baptized with Holy Spirit. Let's look at the next couple of scriptures. Jesus knew He would be finishing His earthly ministry to return to His Father, so He told His disciples about His Holy Spirit who would come and dwell with them. Understand that this process was not just for His disciples but it is necessary for every born-again believer also. If the disciples needed this power to be witnesses for God, than so do we.

John 14:16-18 AMP "And I will ask the Father, and He will give you another Helper (Comforter, Advocate, Intercessor Counselor, Strengthener, Standby), to be with you forever 17 the Spirit of Truth, whom the world cannot receive [and take to its heart] because it does not see Him or know Him, but you know Him because He (the Holy Spirit) remains with you continually and will be in you .18 "I will not leave you as orphans [comfortless, bereaved, and helpless]; I will come [back] to you.

Acts 1:4-5 & 8 AMP *"While being together and eating with them, He (Jesus) commanded them not to leave Jerusalem, but to wait for what the Father had promised, "Of which," He said, "you have heard Me speak. 5 For John baptized with water, but you will be baptized and empowered and united with the Holy Spirit, not long from now 8 But you will receive power and ability when the Holy Spirit comes upon you; and you will be My witnesses [to tell people about Me] both in Jerusalem and in all Judea, and Samaria, and even to the ends of the earth."*

Acts 2:4 AMP *"And they were all filled [that is, diffused throughout their being] with the Holy Spirit and began to speak in other tongues (different languages), as the Spirit was giving them the ability to speak out [clearly and appropriately]."*

If they were all filled with His Holy Spirit, we will also be filled. He will not withhold any good gift from us.

Luke 11:9-13 NKJV *"So I say to you, ask, and it will be given to you; seek, and you will find; knock, and it will be opened to you. 10 For everyone who asks receives, and he who seeks finds, and to him who knocks it will be opened. 11 If a son asks for bread from any father among you, will he give him a stone? Or if he asks for a fish, will he give him a serpent instead of a fish? 12 Or if he asks for an egg, will he offer him a scorpion? 13 If you then, being evil, know how to give good gifts to your children, how much more will your heavenly Father give the Holy Spirit to those who ask Him!"*

Taking Off The Old Man Putting On The New

From these scriptures, we can see that Jesus instructed His disciples to wait for the promised Holy Spirit. Likewise, it is crucial for us to ask for this gift and be baptized with Holy Spirit; (infused) with power.

Also notice that with receiving this gift, you will speak with other tongues. Don't let the tongues throw you off. Speaking in tongues is a healthy practice in our lives. It is an initial sign that you are filled with the gift of Holy Spirit. When we do not know what to pray in English, Holy Spirit will pray for us when we use tongues in prayer. And lastly, it builds you up and edifies your spirit man. It makes you stronger. Are you ready to pray for the baptism of the Holy Spirit?

Prayer: Father, in the name of Jesus, I ask you now to fill me with Holy Spirit with the evidence of speaking in other tongues. I receive Him now by faith in the name of Jesus. I thank you for filling me and I will speak with other tongues, as the Spirit gives me the language. In Jesus' name, Amen.

If you have prayed that prayer, you have received the gift of God's Holy Spirit; infused with power. You may or may not have spoken in other tongues at this time but do not let that discourage you. Just continue to spend time with God because spending quality time with God in prayer is vital. It is in your time alone with Him; that you will feel secure to speak what you feel stirring in your spirit. We are instructed to *"ask and continue to ask Him"* **(Luke 11:13 AMP)**

As a baby Christian, I desperately wanted everything God had for me so I sought for my prayer language until I spoke in tongues. I shocked myself when it happened but I was so glad that I had the evidence that I had been baptized with power.

I'm excited for you! Holy Spirit will guide you into all truth and mature you if you allow Him to.

2 Thessalonians 2:13b AMP *"because God has chosen you from the beginning for salvation through the sanctifying work of the Spirit [that sets you apart for God's purpose] and by your faith in the truth [of God's word that leads you to spiritual maturity]."*

The Value of Your Life In Christ

1 Corinthians 6:20 AMP *"You were bought with a price [you were actually purchased with the precious blood of Jesus and made His own]. So then, honor and glorify God with your body."*

1 Corinthians 6:19-20 NKJV *"Or do you not know that your body is the temple of the Holy Spirit who is in you, whom you have from God, and you are not your own? 20 For you were bought at a price; therefore glorify God in your body and in your spirit, which are God's."*

So from these scriptures, you see that you are the purchased possession of Jesus and very valuable to Him. You are no longer your own, and in this case, that is a very good thing. Unbeknownst to you, you were not your own in your sinful state. In your sinful state, you were a slave to sin, controlled by the devil and you didn't know it. Jesus said it best in:

John 8:34 NKJV *"Most assuredly, I say to you, whoever commits sin is a slave of sin."*

Please listen to this verse from the Message Bible:

John 8:34 MSG *"Jesus said, "I tell you most solemnly that anyone who chooses a life of sin is trapped in a dead-end life and is, in fact, a **slave**. A slave is a transient, who can't come* *and go at will. The Son, though, has an established position, the run of the house. So if the Son sets you free, you are free through and through."*

Romans Chapter 6 drives the point home that we are now free from sin if we choose to be.

Romans 6:6, NLT *says, "We know that our old sinful selves were crucified with Christ so that sin might lose its power in our lives. We are no longer slaves to sin."*

Romans 6:6 MSG *"Could it be any clearer? Our old way of life was nailed to the cross with Christ, a decisive end to that sin-miserable life no longer at sin's every beck and call! What we believe is this: If we get included in Christ's sin-conquering death, we also get included in his life-saving resurrection."*

It was the sin in our lives that the devil used to drive us to do everything that was contrary to what God wanted for us. When we are not aware of the scriptures, we could potentially continue in sin if we don't learn how to take off the old man after being born-again.

Taking Off The Old Man

I have something to say about taking off the old nature. This gesture does not mean you lose your personality. If you have a good personality; pleasant, loving, funny, generous, have a lot of zeal, full of life and everyone enjoys being around you, God does not want that to change. He can use those characteristics. On the other hand, if you have a bad temper, selfish, stingy, and have other ungodly behaviors, that's a different story. You should welcome the change. Remember, the idea is to become

Taking Off The Old Man Putting On The New

like Jesus. We can still have a great life of fun, but we'll allow God to be in charge and not the enemy. Taking off the old man is like changing our clothes. When we look in a mirror and see that our clothes are dirty, we change and put on a clean set of clothes. In the same way, when we see in the Word of God that our old sinful way of living does not line up with how God desires us to live, we have to change our minds to line up with how God does things. Taking off the old man requires us to renew our mind with the assistance of Holy Spirit. It requires educating ourselves with reading His Word and acting on what we read. Here are a few scriptures that make it very clear.

Romans 12:2 KJV *"And do not be conformed to this world: but be ye transformed by the renewing of your mind, that ye may prove what is that good, and acceptable, and perfect, will of God."*

I have shared this scripture before but here is the same scripture from The Message Bible.

Romans 12:2 MSG *"So, here's what I want you to do, God helping you: Take your everyday, ordinary life your sleeping, eating, going-to-work, and walking-around life and place it before God as an offering. Embracing what God does for you is the best thing you can do for him. Don't become so well-adjusted to your culture that you fit into it without even thinking. Instead, fix your attention on God. You'll be changed from the inside out. Readily recognize what he wants from you, and quickly respond to it. Unlike the culture around you, always dragging you down to its level of immaturity, God brings the best out of you, develops well-formed maturity in you.*

Ephesians 4:17-24 GNT *"In the Lord's name, then, I warn you: do not continue to live like the heathen, whose thoughts*

Taking Off The Old Man Putting On The New

are worthless 18 and whose minds are in the dark. They have no part in the life that God gives, for they are completely ignorant and stubborn. 19 They have lost all feeling of shame; they give themselves over to vice and do all sorts of indecent things without restraint. 20 That was not what you learned about Christ! 21 You certainly heard about him, and as his followers, you were taught the truth that is in Jesus. 22 So get rid of your old self, which made you live as you used to the old self that was being destroyed by its deceitful desires. 23 Your hearts and minds must be made completely new, 24 and you must put on the new self, which is created in God's likeness and reveals itself in the true life that is upright and holy."

After we say yes to (our adoption), the salvation plan of God, we become citizens of heaven and should no longer continue in the same way of living. Those who respond in faith to God through a relationship with Jesus Christ have been united with Him.

Paul said in **Galatians 2:20 NKJV** *"I have been crucified with Christ," "and I no longer live, but Christ lives in me."*
He also said in **Colossians 3:3 NKJV** that our lives are *"hidden with Christ in God."*

What do those scriptures mean to us, and how do we apply them to our lives. It means that we have passed from a life of death into life with Christ. We have inherited the change. God no longer sees the old man but the Christ in us. We are hidden. We must simply believe in the gift that God has graciously blessed us with in Christ. The work was done for us when we were *"made righteous." (2 Corinthians 5:21).* Our part is to continue the change and embrace the process, taking an active role in our transformation to be holy (set apart). Being "seated with God in heavenly places in Christ Jesus" **Ephesians 2:6,** is another scripture that conveys to us that we have been elevated from our old life by our relationship with Jesus. We have been translated from darkness into light. That is a gift that we're not able to get anywhere else.

Romans 6:4-6 NKJV says; *"Therefore we were buried with Him through baptism into death, that just as Christ was raised from the dead by the glory of the Father, even so, we also should walk in newness of life. For if we have been united together in the likeness of His death, certainly we also shall be in the likeness of His resurrection, knowing this, that our old man was crucified with Him, that the body of sin might be done away with, that we should no longer be slaves of sin.*

Romans 6:4-6 MSG *When we are lowered into the water, it is like the burial of Jesus; when we are raised up out of the water, it is like the resurrection of Jesus. Each of us is raised into a light-filled world by our Father so that we can see where we're going in our new grace-sovereign country.*
Could it be any clearer? Our old way of life was nailed to the cross with Christ, a decisive end to that sin-miserable life and no longer at sin's every beck and call!

When a person has had a true born-again experience, they will have a desire to please God. It may take time for various reasons, but there will be signs of change. When we receive Jesus and the gift of His Holy Spirit, we have a built-in helper. He is our teacher who teaches us and convicts us but does not condemn us. If we allow Him, He will help us to be free from our old lifestyle, and He will do it a little at a time. He is gentle and kind and does not beat us up over our old nature, but He does nudge us to give up things that will hinder our new life in Christ. All we have to do is say no to the old lifestyle. God is holy, and He desires the same thing from us.

Taking Off The Old Man Putting On The New

Hebrews 12:1 NKJV says to us *"Therefore we also since we are surrounded by so great a cloud of witnesses, let us lay aside every weight and the sin which so easily ensnares us, and let us run with endurance the race that is set before us."*

We have to be vigilant to do our part. Sin will keep us in the same place, ensnared and in bondage. It is a partnership that we have entered into with a Holy God who desires to do great things in and through us.

Leviticus 20:7 NKJV *"Consecrate yourselves, therefore, and be holy, for I am the Lord your God."*

You must change so that you can be the best representatives of our Lord. We cannot properly represent Him if we have not submitted ourselves to His Holy Spirit, who will teach us. It is no longer about you, but all about Jesus being Lord.

2 Corinthians 5:17 NKJV *"Therefore, if anyone is in Christ, he is a new creation; old things have passed away; behold, all things have become new."*

All of our old deeds have been wiped from our slate; the old life is gone. But if we don't understand that very important aspect of the new birth, and begin to renew our mind in the Word of God, we will not change even though God has set us free from sin. It's all about progressively growing in your relationship with Christ, and that is something that should not be taken lightly.

James 1:21-25 NKJV *Therefore, get rid of all moral filth and the evil that is so prevalent and humbly accept the word planted in you, which can save you. 22 Do not merely listen to the word, and so deceive yourselves. Do what it says. 23 Anyone who listens to the word but does not do what it says is*

Taking Off The Old Man Putting On The New

like someone who looks at his face in a mirror 24 and, after looking at himself, goes away and immediately forgets what he looks like. 25 But he who looks into the perfect law of liberty and continues in it, and is not a forgetful hearer but a doer of the work, this one will be blessed in what he does.

So as a believer, receive the truth and let it make you free because all scripture is used to direct us.

2 Timothy 3:16 NKJV tells us that *"All scripture is God-breathed and is useful for teaching, rebuking, correcting and training in righteousness."*

Remember He is our Heavenly Father and just like any father, He must correct, teach and train us so that we are better citizens for His use. If He does not chasten (correct) us, the scripture says that we do not belong to Him *(Hebrews 12:8)* So, as an obedient child of God, take the advice from this next scripture and apply it to your life.

1 John 2:5-6 NIV says *"But if anyone obeys His Word, the love for God is made complete in them. This is how we know we are in Him: Whoever claims to live in Him must live as Jesus did."*

Colossians 3:1-9 NKJV *"If then you were raised with Christ, seek those things which are above where Christ is sitting at the right hand of God. Set your mind on things above not on things on the earth. For you died and your life is hidden with Christ in God. When Christ who is our life appears, then you also will appear with Him in glory. Therefore, put to death your members which are on the earth: fornication, uncleanness, passion, evil desire, and covetousness which is idolatry. Because of these things the wrath of God is coming upon the sons of disobedience, in which you yourselves once walked when you lived in them. But you yourselves are to put*

Taking Off The Old Man Putting On The New

off all these: anger, wrath, malice, blasphemy, filthy language out of your mouth. Do not lie to one another, since you have put off the old man with his deeds."

I love the Word of God because it does not get any clearer than that. If we have been born-again, the character traits that are listed should no longer be a part of our new life in Christ, or at least we should be working to take off those things and working toward holiness (Pure Living). The old man must go only to be replaced by a better you. I didn't realize I was a slave to sin before I was born again. I knew I needed help, but I had no idea that sin was driving me, and that I had no power over it. I was in bondage and didn't even know it. I thank God for *Romans 6:6* that told me that my old self was crucified with Jesus when I said yes to the invitation to be born again (my adoption) and at that time I was free from sin and the weight of it. As I said earlier, I remember feeling the weight of the world lift off of my shoulders, and I felt free. That experience in and of itself was enough to make me want to know more about God and what else He could do in and through my life. As I began my new life, I learned that I had to take part in renewing my mind and learn how to say no to the old way of thinking and that I had the power to do so. Oh yes, it was a conscious decision to accept that I needed to change some things in my life. But remember, God gave me His Holy Spirit as my helper to teach me what I needed to know. I did rely on Him. I would confess scriptures such as **Philippians 4:13** that says *"I can do all things through Christ who strengthens me."*

This scripture gave me hope because I put my confidence in God's Word and Holy Spirit to help me.

John 14:16-18 NKJV *"And I will pray the Father, and He will give you another Helper, that He may abide with you* *forever the Spirit of truth, whom the world cannot receive, because it neither sees Him nor knows Him; but you know Him, for He dwells with you and will be in you. I will not leave you orphans; I will come to you."*

Notice that these scriptures are written to the believer. Let me reinforce some things about Holy Spirit. He is God's Holy Spirit, and His function in our lives is to lead and guide us into all truth. He is our Helper, Comforter, Advocate, Intercessor Counselor, Strengthener (power) and Standby. He should not be taken lightly because our destiny depends on Him. Holy Spirit belongs exclusively to the believer, and He is made available to aid us in us our spiritual growth. I can't stress that enough. We must allow Him to teach us so that we can fully understand what He is accomplishing, in and through our lives. It is said that "Jesus Must Be Lord of All or He's Not Lord at All." That is a sobering thought.

Putting on the New Man

I have talked about taking off the old man so now let's look at what the scripture says about putting on the new man. In our newness of life, we have been instructed what to do. Let us look at:

Colossians 3:12 NKJV *"Therefore, as the elect of God, holy and beloved, put on tender mercies, kindness, humility, meekness, longsuffering; 13 bearing with one another, and forgiving one another, if anyone has a complaint against another; even as Christ forgave you, so you also must do.14 But above all these things put on love, which is the bond of perfection. 15 And let the peace of God rule in your hearts, to which also you were called in one body; and be thankful. 16 Let the Word of Christ dwell in you richly in all wisdom,*

Taking Off The Old Man Putting On The New

teaching and admonishing one another in psalms and hymns and spiritual songs, singing with grace in your hearts to the Lord. 17 And whatever you do in word or deed, do all in the name of the Lord Jesus, giving thanks to God the Father through Him."

This verse says it all. With Holy Spirit helping us, we can accomplish this. To ignore these instructions and others like them is to forfeit the process of our new life.

Ephesians 4:23-24 NKJV *"And be renewed in the spirit of your mind, 24 and that you put on the new man which was created according to God, in true righteousness and holiness."*

I believe these instructional scriptures are not known, or they are ignored by a great deal of the Body of Christ because of the behavior that is still displayed by some brothers and sisters in Christ. When the scripture tells us to take off the old man and put on the new man, that means there should be a change in our lives. We should no longer participate in ungodly activities that we were once involved in. If we can't figure out what the immoral behaviors are, the conviction of Holy Spirit will lead you into all truth--just don't ignore the nudge. As ambassadors of Christ, *let's "abstain from every appearance of evil." (1 Thessalonians 5:22).* We live in a time when evil is called good and good is called evil. For example; living together before marriage. People think it's crazy to not live together before marriage, but how does God feel about that behavior? That is not the will of God for our lives, but some believers do it anyway. That behavior will destroy your witness. I believe part of the problem is that people just don't know what God has said in His Word. As believers, we must know the difference between good and evil as God sees it. We have His Holy Spirit to lead and guide us. Remember, if you prayed to receive Jesus, He is there and Holy Spirit is waiting to assist you. A good Bible teaching church is also important. Unfortunately, not all churches teach the truth of God's Word.

Romans 13:14 NKJV *tells us "But put on the Lord Jesus Christ, and make no provision for the flesh, to fulfill its lusts."*

So how do we put on the Lord Jesus Christ? Well, this process happens at salvation but must be an on-going process in the life of the believer. Putting on the Lord Jesus Christ is identifying with Jesus and everything He does. It is being clothed, with His attitude, His habits, His disposition; some of which are submission, obedience, and the nine fruit of the Spirit; love, joy, peace, longsuffering, kindness, goodness, faithfulness, gentleness, and self-control.

Isaiah 61:10AMP *For He has clothed me with garments of salvation, and He has covered me with a robe of righteousness,*

After taking off our old nature, we have to replace it with Christ-likeness. It is a deliberate, on purpose act, that continues as we begin to surround ourselves with like-minded people that are going in the same direction as we are along with spending time with God in Prayer and reading His Word. These instructions will be repeated throughout this book; it is the only way. Years ago the acronym "WWJD" came out. "What Would Jesus Do?" Christ-likeness is what we as Christians are striving for; to be like Christ. We have to remember that people are watching us, but more importantly, God is watching us. Our behavior speaks volumes. People may not know the scripture in the Bible, but they are reading our lives. They know the type of behavior that we should display. It is our responsibility to pattern our new lives after Jesus and be His example in the world.

Taking Off The Old Man Putting On The New

Romans 13:12-13 AMP tells us *"The night [this present evil age] is almost gone and the day [of Christ's return] is almost here. So let us fling away the works of darkness and put on the [full] armor of light. 13 Let us conduct ourselves properly and honorably as in the [light of] day, not in carousing and drunkenness, not in sexual promiscuity and irresponsibility, not in quarreling and jealousy."*

Jesus said in ***John 8:12 NKJV*** *"I am the light of the world. He who follows Me shall not walk in darkness, but have the light of life."*

Putting on the armor of light is the same as putting on the Lord Jesus Christ; it is a deliberate decision to behave in a godly manner. When we consistently operate in a godly manner, we become the light to those around us. In some cases, we become the person that people confide in. They come to us for prayer because they see that we don't get involved in the gossip so they know that they can trust us. Since Jesus rescued us from the dominion of darkness, we can live as children of light, and light dispels darkness. This doesn't mean that we won't make mistakes, but it does mean that our new normal should reflect our life in Christ. Our allegiance is no longer to the world but God.

According to ***Philippians 2:15 NKJV*** *"That you may become blameless and harmless, children of God without fault in the midst of a crooked and perverse generation, among whom you shine as lights in the world."*

Matthew 5:13-14 *"You are the salt of the earth; but if the salt loses its flavor, how shall it be seasoned? It is then good for nothing but to be thrown out and trampled underfoot by men.*

Taking Off The Old Man Putting On The New

You are the light of the world. A city that is set on a hill cannot be hidden".

Not only are we called to be light in the world, but also salt of the earth. Let's look at how Believers compare to salt. We know that salt is a preservative and gives flavor to enhance food. In the same way, Christians should stand out as those who "enhance" the life of those around them. Christians, which are being led by Holy Spirit, should influence the world for good, having a positive effect on them.

I can only imagine that all of this information could be extremely overwhelming, but it does not have to be. Take it in stride and continue to grow. For me, I was constantly seeking God so I was always excited about this kind of information. Once you have decided to serve God, remember that He's a kind and gentle God, I can't stress that enough. He understands who we are as individuals, and that is how He deals with us.

Hebrews 4:15 NIV tells us *"For we do not have a high priest who is unable to empathize with our weaknesses, but we have one who has been tempted in every way, just as we are yet he did not sin. ¹⁶ Let us then approach God's throne of grace with confidence, so that we may receive mercy and find grace to help us in our time of need.*

Hebrews 2:17 NKJV *"Therefore, in all things He had to be made like His brethren,(mankind) that He might be a merciful and faithful High Priest in things pertaining to God, to make propitiation for the sins of the people. ¹⁸ For in that He Himself has suffered, being tempted, He is able to aid those who are tempted."*

I feel it is important to continue to share scriptures like these because we continue to see the provision that was made on our

Taking Off The Old Man Putting On The New

behalf. He set us up to win in every area of our lives. We can have confidence in approaching Him in prayer about our weaknesses. These verses tells us that our sin nature is why He came. He sympathizes with us because He experienced everything that we experience and He conquered it--and we can also. Here is one more verse to encourage you.

1 Corinthians 10:13 NKJV *"No temptation has overtaken you except such as is common to man; but God is faithful, who will not allow you to be tempted beyond what you are able, but with the temptation will also make the way of escape, that you may be able to bear it."*

We have all the help we need to live a life pleasing to our Heavenly Father.

So, Why Are We Here?

That is a good question. Why are we born into this life only to die 70, 80 or 90 years later? Unfortunately, that is exactly what happens to a good number of people who are born into this life. They are oblivious to why they are here. It's been said that the cemetery is the riches real estate in the world because so many people have taken all the gifts God blessed them with, to be used by Him, to the grave. Well, here it is! We are here to worship, honor, and glorify God with our lifestyle.

Romans 12:1 AMP *"Therefore I urge you, brothers and sisters, by the mercies of God, to present your bodies [dedicating all of yourselves, set apart] as a living sacrifice, holy and well-pleasing to God, which is your rational (logical, intelligent) act of worship."*

We are here for the sole purpose of glorifying God with our lives; carrying out the purpose and plan that He has planned for us from the foundation of the world. Once we realize why we are here, we must be obedient to what God wants of us. Scripture informs us in many places why we are here. To start, *Jeremiah 1:5* tells us that God set us apart for Himself and that He has a plan for everyone that comes into this earth. I have shared this scripture before but it bears repeating.

Jeremiah 1:5 AMP *"Before I formed you in the womb I knew you [and approved of you as My chosen instrument], And before you were born I consecrated you [to Myself as My own]; I have appointed you as a prophet to the nations."*

WOW!! Our arrival here on earth was no mystery to God. He made us just the way He brought us here for His intended purpose. Are you being used by God, for His glory?

So, Why Are We Here?

If not, why not? You might say, yes I am being used, but do you understand that it has to be on God's terms and not yours? All the provisions for us to be great in Him have already been made. Submitting ourselves to the Lordship of Jesus Christ is what we must do. The invitation was extended, our adoption was made sure, now He has an amazing future planned for us, and He is going to make it happen. So right here, I will introduce Grace.

Grace

Let us talk about grace. What is grace? Grace is "God's unmerited **favor**" according to the amplified version of the bible. Unmerited favor was my first introduction to grace. But grace means so much more than that. But keeping it simple so that you can get an understanding, it means God's supernatural ability on our natural ability. It means that God will do through us what we cannot do on our own. He will use us for His purpose and plan, and we will experience the pleasure of Him using us. Let's go a little further. We all know what a favor is because we ask it of our friends and family when we ask them, "can you do me a favor"? When we ask them to do us a favor, it is because, for whatever reason, we cannot perform that task ourselves. Breaking it down some more, let's look at the meaning in Dictionary.com. **Favor is something done or granted out of good will; a kind act; A state of being approved or held in regard; Excessive kindness or unfair partiality; preferential treatment; A gift bestowed as a token of goodwill, kind regard, and love.** So creating a sentence from this meaning, I can say that, when we become God's children, He holds us in kind regard. He has granted us His favor which is preferential treatment; unfair partiality, to accomplish His Will. He extends His excessive acts of kindness, and most importantly, His love and goodwill.

So, Why Are We Here?

How was that? I hope from the definition, and by inserting it into a sentence, I did justice in explaining favor, which translates to grace. We can expect and access the grace of God when we need it. He is always present in our lives showing up just to show His favor. Remember, it's based on His excessive kindness and preferential treatment. "Favor ain't fair" is a saying in Christendom that simply means "unfair partiality; preferential treatment." He enables us to do whatever needs to be done for His glory, and for our pleasure as well. That being said, not everyone can say that they have God's favor. Every living creature will experience God's goodness because He is good, but only His children will know His unmerited favor (grace).

In these next scriptures, take note of the grace that's been extended to us.

Ephesians 2:4-8 NKJV *" But God, who is rich in mercy, because of His great love for us,* <u>*even when we were dead in transgressions, made us alive*</u> *5* <u>*with Christ it is by grace you have been saved.*</u> *6* <u>*And God raised us up with Christ and seated us with Him in the heavenly realms in Christ Jesus,*</u> *7 in order that in the coming ages He might show the incomparable riches of His grace, expressed in His kindness to us in Christ Jesus. 8* <u>*For it is by grace you have been saved*</u>*, through faith and this is not from yourselves, it is the gift of God.*

I wanted you to see that scripture because of His love for us and the gift of His grace. But these next scriptures say that His grace keeps on coming.

2 Corinthians 12:9 Amplified Bible (AMP) *but He has said to me, "My grace is sufficient for you [My lovingkindness and My mercy are more than enough always available regardless*

So, Why Are We Here?

of the situation]; for [My] power is being perfected [and is completed and shows itself most effectively] in [your] weakness." Therefore, I will all the more gladly boast in my weaknesses, so that the power of Christ [may completely enfold me and] may dwell in me.

Just in case you didn't comprehend what this is saying, when we acknowledge our weaknesses and/or inabilities to God, He says to us, I've got you.

James 4:6 AMPC *But He gives us more and more grace power of the Holy Spirit, to meet this evil tendency and all others fully). That is why He says, God sets Himself against the proud and haughty, but gives grace [continually] to the lowly (those who are humble enough to receive it).*

Psalms 5:12 AMP tells us *"For You, O Lord, bless the righteous man [the one who is in right standing with You]; You surround him with favor as with a shield."*

I know you were encouraged by those scriptures. I shared them to help you see that favor (grace) is not lacking. We can expect that God's grace is made available to us from now until we go to be with Him in heaven. He will not change His mind concerning His plan for our lives. He planned our lives before we were born into this world. We have to be willing to cooperate with His plan, and He promises to accomplish it through us, by His Grace.

I encourage you to find resources about the Grace of God. There are teachings on Grace that go into great depth and bring out so much more clarity.

We Are His Representatives In The Earth

Romans 8:29 AMP *"For those whom He foreknew [and loved and chose beforehand], He also predestined to be **conformed to the image of His Son** [and ultimately share in His complete sanctification], so that He would be the firstborn [the most beloved and honored] among many believers."*

Why does He want us to be conformed to the image of His Son? So that we can represent Him in the earth. He is no different from any other parent who wants their children to represent them in a good way. My mother-in-law, the late Delores E. Pryde, would always tell Bud (my husband) "remember who you are" when he left the house. He represented the household when he was in public, and in the same way, we represent God in the earth. When we are conformed to His image, our lifestyle will show it. We will be the peculiar person in the group, and it will be evident that we are sanctified (set apart) for God. I heard a story of a pastor who was also a businessman. He would have to sit in roundtable meetings where his colleagues would have alcoholic beverages. He said that he would not even drink a glass of water because it looked like it could be vodka. That might sound a little extreme, but he cared more about how it would look to someone who entered the room and didn't see him pour the water. In his mind, he remembered that:

1 Thessalonians 5:22 KJV tells us to *"abstain from all appearances of evil."*

He left no room for error because he wanted to represent God wherever he was. We all should feel the same way because we are here representing Him. Scripture instructs us not to cause others to stumble by what we allow. (1 Corinthian 8:9)

So, Why Are We Here?

I'm still taking about why we are here.

Psalms 139:16 NET *"Your eyes saw me when I was inside the womb. All the days ordained for me were recorded in your scroll before one of them came into existence."*

This says to us that God planned for our arrival. He had His eyes on us from the beginning of time. He knew exactly what He planned for our lives. That is so exciting; to think that we were in the thoughts and plans of All Mighty God.

Ephesians 1:4-5 NKJV says *"just as He chose us in Him before the foundation of the world, that we should be holy and without blame before Him in love, 5 having predestined us to adoption as sons by Jesus Christ to Himself, according to the good pleasure of His will."*

Ephesians 2:10 NKJV *"For we are His workmanship, created in Christ Jesus for good works, which God prepared beforehand that we should walk in them."*

It is crystal clear that God's plan for our lives are waiting for us. All of us won't preach the gospel in the church pulpit, but He does want us to honor Him with our life in our neighborhood, on our jobs, and before our family members and friends. We are equipped with a gift(s) that He's placed on the inside of us just for His purpose. The gifts that we possess are not for us, although we do get to enjoy them. God uses them for the people who we will minister to. Let's look at the life of a praise and worship singer. They get to enjoy singing, but the gift is ultimately used to create an atmosphere to usher people into the presence of God, where He can begin to minister to the people individually. God anoints the singer, and the people can feel God's presence through their gift. Make no mistake; if you feel God's presence in the assembly,

So, Why Are We Here?

it's God enabling them and not them enabling themselves. It is God's anointing, and in that transfer, God gets the glory, and the singer is also blessed by being used by God. So please remember that the gifts are from God to be used by God to bless others. After the Lord uses me, and others want to compliment me, my words to them are "TO GOD BE ALL THE GLORY!" I do that because I know that I am His vessel being used of Him. *"If a man, therefore, purge himself from these, he shall be a vessel unto honor, sanctified, and meet for the master's use, and prepared unto every good work." (2 Timothy 2:21)* I will not pat myself on the back, but I do experience so much pleasure in fulfilling His purpose.

I pray that this information will give you a new awareness of God and somehow make you desire the life that I am writing about. Don't forfeit the purpose and plan of God for your life by allowing your old nature to dictate to you how you will live your new life once you know He has a plan for your life. Our goal is to hear Him say, *"well done good and faithful servant" (Matthew 25:21).* We have to follow His system because anything else would be in vain. There are all kinds of belief systems about Jesus, salvation, and heaven. It is a very delicate subject, but Christians must talk about it. After all, "the great commission is our main mission" and why we are on this earth. That is a quote from my Pastor, Apostle Mike Freeman. He also said, "we are this earth's answer." He is right because somebody has to share it. We have the answer. As I said in chapter one, God takes it seriously, so I must share the gospel with those around me.

Romans 10:14 NKJV *How then shall they call on Him in whom they have not believed? And how shall they believe in Him of whom they have not heard? And how shall they hear without a preacher? ¹⁵And how shall they preach unless they are sent? As it is written: "How beautiful are the feet of those*

So, Why Are We Here?

who preach the gospel of peace, Who bring glad tidings of good things!"

When I read this scripture, I see how valuable God's children are to Him. He is sending us out to present the Good News to those who don't know. No believer should ever wonder why they are here. Our purpose is written throughout the scripture. I wish I could say with certainty that all of my loved ones who departed this life went to heaven but I can't. In fact, I'm almost certain that some of them have never heard the Good News of Jesus, and how He came to be their personal Lord and Savior. I say that because they didn't give their children the inheritance of salvation, knowing Jesus as their Lord and Savior. What parent will have the saving knowledge of Jesus Christ and not minister it to their children? What parent would know the ramification of sin and not warn their children? But I hold onto hope that somehow, someway, they heard the gospel message before they departed this earth. This is why we must renew our minds. I'm taking it personally because it is my responsibility to share Jesus, and not just share but to disciple them also. As Christians, we are the sent ones, His representatives. I'm still talking about why we are here. There is so much more to life than being born, doing your own thing and then dying. As I shared a few paragraphs back. We are born with specific gifts and callings that God has put there for His purpose.

Psalms 139:14-16 TLB *"Thank you for making me so wonderfully complex! It is amazing to think about. Your workmanship is marvelous and how well I know it. 15 You were there while I was being formed in utter seclusion! 16 <u>You saw me before I was born and scheduled each day of my life before I began to breathe. Every day was recorded in Your Book!</u>"*

So, Why Are We Here?

God planned our lives out before we were born, but if we never take our adoption seriously, we will never know what great things He has for us. I only have one question for you, how many appointments have you missed by not being in fellowship with God? I have asked myself that same question, and unfortunately, it has been many because of doubt and unbelief.

Ephesians 2:10 AMP *"For we are God's [own] handiwork (His workmanship), recreated in Christ Jesus, [born anew] that we may do those good works which God predestined (planned beforehand) for us [taking paths which He prepared ahead of time], that we should walk in them [living the good life which He prearranged and made ready for us to live]."*

I love this scripture!!! God prepared a good life ahead of time for us to walk in, but it is up to us to find that path. Destiny is something that has to be discovered, and many people will go to their graves having not discovered their purpose. They may go to heaven but miss fulfilling destiny. The scripture talks about gifts and callings. (Ephesians 4 and 1 Corinthians 12) In your study, refer to those books of the Bible. There are those who know their purpose. There are those whose gift(s) are evident, but if it's not submitted to the Lordship of Jesus Christ, to be used for the kingdom, it's in vain because God doesn't get the glory. I'm reminded once again of the gifted singer. Their gift is meant to be used for God's glory if they desire His approval. This is not to say that they can't sing for their own pleasure or make a living singing, I don't believe that is the case at all but they should be conscious of why they were gifted to sing. It has to be done according to His way.

2 Timothy 1: 9 AMP *"For He delivered us and saved us and called us with a holy calling [a calling that leads to a consecrated life a life set apart life of purpose], not because of*

So, Why Are We Here?

our works [or because of any personal merit we could do nothing to earn this], but because of His own purpose and grace [His amazing, undeserved favor] which was granted to us in Christ Jesus before the world began [eternal ages ago],"

However, by the time some people come into the knowledge of God's plan for their lives, they have gone years conforming to their surroundings of non-Christianity and their own fleshly desires, it takes so much time to accept the Kingdom of God (God's ways of doing things). This is not the case for all but the case for most. I have seen transformations that seem to have manifested overnight, where a person embraces the ways of God and resisted their old nature with no problem. They grow up to become vessels of honor. If a person is not "all in" from the start, it is going to be a chore to operate in God's Kingdom. You have to make up in your mind that you are going to separate yourself from the world to get to know God; His ways and His thoughts because in the Kingdom of God, we operate differently than in the world system.

Isaiah 55:8 NKJV *"For My thoughts* are not your thoughts, Nor are your ways My ways,' says the Lord."

It is not until we are born again that we can take on the thoughts of God and understand His ways. He has planned things that will blow our minds, but we have to trust Him. As I shared before, *"Eye has not seen, nor ear heard, Nor have entered into the heart of man the things which God has prepared for those who love Him."* **(1 Corinthians 2:9)**

We can possess the inheritance of God just as Abraham did, by walking by faith and not by sight. I am reminded of Abraham when God told him to leave everything he knew.

So, Why Are We Here?

Hebrews 11:8 NKJV *"By faith Abraham obeyed when he was called to go out to the place which he would receive as an inheritance. And he went out, not knowing where he was going. By faith he dwelt in the land of promise as in a foreign country, dwelling in tents with Isaac and Jacob, the heirs with him of the same promise."*

Understanding Faith

We have looked at grace, now let's talk a little about faith because grace and faith work together. What is faith?

According to ***Hebrews 11:1-2 (TLB)*** *"It is the confident assurance that something we want is going to happen. It is the certainty that what we hope for is waiting for us, even though we cannot see it up ahead."*

Taking small steps, This is saying; in God, we have to have confident assurance with certainty that what we hope for (His Grace) is waiting for us. The amount of **grace** we receive from God is based on how much **faith** we have in **His** ability, and that is across the board with everything we receive from Him. In other words, in the Kingdom of God, we have to believe it before we see it. I want to share another scripture that demonstrates how Abraham believed God.

Genesis 22:1-14 NKJV *Now it came to pass after these things that God tested Abraham, and said to him, "Abraham!" And he said, "Here I am." ² Then He said, "Take now your son, your only son Isaac, whom you love, and go to the land of Moriah, and offer him there as a burnt offering on one of the mountains of which I shall tell you." ³ So Abraham rose early in the morning and saddled his donkey, and took two of his young men with him, and Isaac his son; and he split the wood*

So, Why Are We Here?

for the burnt offering, and arose and went to the place of which God had told him. ⁴ Then on the third day Abraham lifted his eyes and saw the place afar off. ⁵ And Abraham said to his young men, "Stay here with the donkey; the lad and I will go yonder and worship, and we will come back to you." ⁶ So Abraham took the wood of the burnt offering and laid it on Isaac his son; and he took the fire in his hand, and a knife, and the two of them went together. ⁷ But Isaac spoke to Abraham his father and said, "My father!" And he said, "Here I am, my son." Then he said, "Look, the fire and the wood, but where is the lamb for a burnt offering?" ⁸ And Abraham said, "My son, God will provide for Himself the lamb for a burnt offering." So the two of them went together. ⁹ Then they came to the place of which God had told him. And Abraham built an altar there and placed the wood in order; and he bound Isaac his son and laid him on the altar, upon the wood. ¹⁰ And Abraham stretched out his hand and took the knife to slay his son. ¹¹ But the Angel of the LORD called to him from heaven and said, "Abraham, Abraham!" So he said, "Here I am." ¹² And He said, "Do not lay your hand on the lad, or do anything to him; for now I know that you fear God, since you have not withheld your son, your only son, from Me." ¹³ Then Abraham lifted his eyes and looked, and there behind him was a ram caught in a thicket by its horns. So Abraham went and took the ram, and offered it up for a burnt offering instead of his son. ¹⁴ And Abraham called the name of the place, The-LORD-Will-Provide; as it is said to this day, "In the Mount of the LORD it shall be provided."

Abraham was confident in God's ability and faithfulness. Scripture says that he concluded that God was able to raise his son up from the dead if indeed he had to slay him. But instead, because of his obedience to God, God showed in His provision. We can be encouraged to know that God is no

So, Why Are We Here?

respecter of persons; what He did for Abraham He will do for us.

After reading that story, do you have confident assurance (faith) that God will show up for you? If not, you must read the Word of God until your faith is built up to believe it. Faith comes by hearing the Word of God. Meditate on the Word until you have confident assurance. Once that happens, nothing will be able to shake your faith. This scripture is telling us that we can trust that God has already made provision for us. The world wants to see it with their natural eyes before they believe it but that is not how the Kingdom of God works.

"For we walk by faith, not by sight [living our lives in a manner consistent with our confident belief in God's promises]." **(2 Corinthians 5:7)** I mentioned earlier that this is not a name it and claim it act, but trusting in God. Remember our faith is in His ability, not our ability. I want to share *Romans 4*. It is an account of Abraham and how he believed God in spite of his old age and Sarah's dead womb.

Romans 4:18-22 NKJV *18 who, contrary to hope, in hope believed, so that he became the father of many nations, according to what was spoken, "So shall your descendants be.] 19 And not being weak in faith, he did not consider his own body, already dead (since he was about a hundred years old), and the deadness of Sarah's womb. 20 He did not waver at the promise of God through unbelief but was strengthened in faith, giving glory to God, 21 and being fully convinced that what He (God) had promised He was also able to perform. 22 And therefore "it was accounted to him for righteousness."*

Abraham didn't waver but instead was strengthened in faith. That says to me that Abraham was convinced that God would deliver on the promise He made to him. He believed God, and it was accounted to him as righteousness. We can have the

So, Why Are We Here?

same outcome in our lives. Why? Because our confidence is in God and His ability and not in our ability.

Matthew 9:29 AMP *"According to your faith [your trust and confidence in My power and My ability to heal] it will be done to you."*

To trust God in this capacity, you have to get His Word in your heart so that when any crisis arises in your life, you have confidence in declaring His Word over the situation.

Romans 10:17 NIV says that *"Consequently, faith comes from hearing the message, and the message is heard through the word about Christ."*

The more we hear the Word taught, the more faith we'll have in His ability. We have to know that whatever God promises in His Word, He will perform it in our lives. *(Isaiah 55:11)* I don't know how you feel about that, but trust me it takes a mind shift to believe that the promises of God will happen in your life when you are not used to functioning that way, and especially if you don't see the promise immediately.

Hebrews 11:6 NKJV tells us, *"But without faith, it is impossible to please Him, for he who comes to God must believe that He is and that He is a rewarder of those who diligently seek Him."*

The rewards are the gifts, abilities, anointing, healings, favor, and so much more. We have to believe that He is who He says He is and trust that He can do what He says He can do. This next scripture will encourage you.

Mark 9:23-24 NKJV *Jesus said to him, "If you can believe, all things are possible to him who believes."Immediately the* *father of the child cried out and said with tears, **"Lord, I believe; help my unbelief!"***

I love the response of the father to Jesus' statement. He said, "Lord, I believe but help my unbelief." He recognized that he was lacking in faith. I believe we all experience that at some point as babes and mature Christians. We are all at different levels in our faith walk. The Bible speaks of weak faith, strong faith, little faith, shipwreck faith, and so on. This next scripture implies that we don't need much faith at all to believe.

Matthew 17:20 AMP *He said to them, Because of the littleness of your faith [that is, your lack of firmly relying trust]. For truly I say to you, if you have faith [that is living] like a grain of mustard seed, you can say to this mountain, Move from here to yonder place, and it will move; and nothing will be impossible to you.*

I don't know if you've ever seen a mustard seed, but it is not very big at all. That helps us know that God wants us to put our trust in Him.

Romans 12:3 tells us that *"God has dealt to every man the measure of faith."*

That simply means that we all start with the same amount. It is up to us how it is developed. Faith is like a muscle that has to be developed. We have to read our bibles, pray, and go to church to develop our faith just like we go to the gym to develop our muscles/bodies.

Habakkuk 2:4 AMP *"The righteous will live by **his** faith [in the true God]."*

So, Why Are We Here?

There is so much more to learn about faith. I just wanted to bring awareness to how important it is in the life of the believer. I encourage you to study on Faith. We can't be built up enough in faith.

As you are reading the passages of scripture throughout this book, I pray that you are encouraged to know how much God loves you. He offers you a life of adventure, but you have to be willing to **believe it and receive it by faith**. Perhaps you feel like I did and don't know how to begin. Ask your Heavenly Father to help you. He knows where you are in your faith walk and He is ready and willing to help you.

I'm convinced that many Christians miss the blessings of God because they don't step out in blind faith to believe God and receive what He has already prepared for them. I have to admit that it has taken me a long time to trust God in some areas of my life. But it doesn't have to take long for you. Taking that leap of faith is necessary if we are to realize the greatness of God in our lives. He is our wonderful Heavenly Father who will not let us fail. I spent many of my Christian years playing it safe. But I have taken a leap of faith to write this book and start a business and I do believe there is more.
I can't say this enough, our confidence must be in Him and not ourselves. I hear people say all the time *that "I walk by faith and not by sight"* **(2 Corinthians 5:7),** but real faith walkers understand that they are called to do things that are out of their scope and can't be done in and of themselves. They know how to access the grace of God through faith in His ability.

Daniel 11:32 NKJV tells us, *"but the people who know their God shall be strong, and carry out great exploits."*

Whether the exploit is a work ordained by God for His Kingdom or a desire of our own heart, He has given us the

So, Why Are We Here?

ability to do it. I want to end this chapter by saying, now that you know why you're here let's go on to maturity in renewing our minds so that we can be fit vessels for our Heavenly Father that we may glorify Him in the earth.

The Dangers of Not Renewing Your Mind:

We have been instructed to *"renew our minds"* **(Romans 12:2)**. But what happens when we don't renew our minds? Does it mean that we are not saved? No, it does not mean that we are not saved. It means that we will be what the Bible calls carnal, which means worldly. We get born again, and that is as far as we go in our new life in Christ. It is like being born in the natural and never developing or growing up to be an adult. We remain babies, always having to be pampered, doing nothing except being fed, being carried and crying to get our way. In other words, useless to the Kingdom of God. We never developed a relationship with The Lord Jesus Christ to become a son. A son in the kingdom is a gender-neutral term. A son is someone that matures and gains an understanding of their purpose in the Kingdom of God. They are growing and learning to operate in their purpose so that God can get glory from their life. *Hebrews 6* talks about the peril of not progressing.

Hebrews 6:1-8 NIV *"Therefore let us move beyond the elementary teachings about Christ and be taken forward to maturity, not laying again the foundation of repentance from acts that lead to death, and of faith in God, 2 instruction about cleansing rites, the laying on of hands, the resurrection of the dead, and eternal judgment. 3 And God permitting, we will do so. 4 It is impossible for those who have once been enlightened, who have tasted the heavenly gift, who have shared in the Holy Spirit, 5 who have tasted the goodness of the word of God and the powers of the coming age 6 and who have fallen away, to be brought back to repentance. To their loss,* **they are crucifying the Son of God all over again an**

subjecting him to public disgrace. 7 Land that drinks in the rain are often falling on it and that produces a crop useful to those for whom it is farmed receives the blessing of God. 8 But land that produces thorns and thistles is worthless and is in danger of being cursed. In the end, it will be burned."

After we are born again, we have to plant the Word of God in our heart and grow up. We have to let Christ dwell in our hearts through faith; being rooted and grounded in love. He wants us to be filled with all of the fullness of God. **(Ephesians 3:17)** If being filled with all the fullness of God is not your aim from the onset of your salvation, I promise you that the enemy is excited about your decision. Because we have lived our lives in agreement with the world system before salvation, the old man is not going to just drop off of us; we have to work at it. Look at this warning.

Genesis 4:7 NKJV *"If you do what is right, will you not be accepted? But if you do not do what is right, sin is crouching at your door; it desires to have you,* **but you must rule over it.***"*

In order to rule over the old sinful nature, renewing your mind to the Word of God is the only way and repenting when we have missed the mark. This next scripture helped me understand that playing with sin is something that I just did not want to do.

Matthew 12:43-45 NLT *"When an evil spirit leaves a person, it goes into the desert, seeking rest but finding none.* ⁴⁴ *Then it says, 'I will return to the person I came from.' So it returns and finds its former home empty, swept, and in order.* ⁴⁵ *Then the spirit finds seven other spirits more evil than itself, and they all enter the person and live there. And so that person is* *worse off than before. That will be the experience of this evil generation."*

Now, I'm not implying that we are all full of unclean spirits. No, that is not what I'm saying. However, it's possible that if you were involved in certain activities such as the occult and a long life of heavy drug and alcohol usage, it's possible that you've opened doors to allow evil spirits to come in. Again, I'm not saying that everyone who has delved into those activities are demon possessed but you need to know that those are ways that doors are open in our lives to unclean spirits. Those are just a couple of ways that they can enter.

Now I want to say that when Jesus takes up residency in your spirit and you are filled with Holy Spirit, you cannot be demon possessed. *If the Son makes you free, you are free indeed (John 8:36).* So, once you have been set free, you have to renew your mind and learn how to close the spiritual doors and keep them closed so that you are not giving the enemy a legal right to be in your life. I know this information can be overwhelming but this is the kind of information you need to know, and work into your new regiment so that you can make intelligent decisions about your lifestyle.

2 Timothy 2:15 AMP tells us to *"Study and do your best to present yourself to God approved, a workman [tested by trial] who has no reason to be ashamed, accurately handling and skillfully teaching the word of truth."*

Don't be the person who gets saved and excited about God for a season and then stops growing. If you are not growing, you are drifting back to your old ways, and the devil is waiting to put you in bondage again. God depends on us to grow past the baby stage of our new life. We have to separate ourselves for the sole purpose of getting acquainted with God and His ways.

The Dangers Of Not Renewing Your Mind

This does not mean that we isolate ourselves from the world, but it does mean that a time of separation from our normal activities is necessary so that we can *"draw near to God and He will draw near to you"* **(James 4:8)**. We have to give Him that time and space to minister to us as only He can after we say yes to the covenant relationship that we've entered into with Him. As in any new covenant relationship, (marriage) you spend quality time getting to know each other. Intimacy is important to any marriage relationship. Read these next few verses of scripture with enthusiasm, and don't allow the devil to tell you that God doesn't want you to have any more fun. Scripture commands us;

2 Corinthians 6:17 *"to come out from among them and touch not the unclean thing, and I will receive you."*

He wants us to be holy because He is holy.

2 Corinthians 7:1 MSG *"--- let's make a clean break with everything that defiles or distracts us, both within and without. Let's make our entire lives fit and holy temples for the worship of God.*

Paul admonishes us in ***2 Corinthians 6:14-16*** *"Do not be unequally yoked together with unbelievers. For what fellowship has righteousness with lawlessness? And what communion has the light with darkness? 15 And what accord has Christ with Belial? (Satan) Or what part has a believer with an unbeliever? 16 And what agreement has the temple of God with idols? For you are the temple of the living God."*

What does it mean to be unequally yoked? It simply means that a believer and an unbeliever might not be on the same page with how they want to do business. It could be possible that they are going in two different directions. The unbeliever,

The Dangers Of Not Renewing Your Mind

in most cases, is swayed toward the world's system and that leaves the believer in a compromising position if they are not strong enough to sway the unbeliever into God's system which is a relationship with Jesus. For instance, A born-again Christian should take into consideration whether or not they should marry an unbeliever because they, more than likely, will not have the same value system in some areas of their relationship. For example, the tithe. The believer understands the principle of the tithe, whereas, the unbeliever may not, thus creating a conflict in the relationship. I had that issue in my own marriage with the tithe. Bud didn't mind helping people with his money but to give a tenth of our income to the church was challenging to him. After he received Jesus as his Lord and Savior and renewed his mind to the Word of God, he had no problem submitting to the will of God in that area. Now, he understands that he can't out give God and we are truly blessed. Also, business partners could envision strategies for their business from two different angles. Which partner will prevail in the quest to be heard? Those are just two example of what could potentially happen when two parties are going in different directions. We can't compromise; not because God is mean but because He wants to protect us.

Amos 3:3 KJV *"Can two walk together, except they be agreed?"*

Romans 12:1-2 in the Message Bible bears repeating.

Romans 12:1-2 MSG *"So here's what I want you to do, God helping you: Take your everyday, ordinary life your sleeping, eating, going-to-work, and walking-around life and place it before God as an offering. Embracing what God does for you is the best thing you can do for him. Don't become so well-adjusted to your culture that you fit into it without even thinking. Instead, fix your attention on God. You'll be changed*

The Dangers Of Not Renewing Your Mind

from the inside out. Readily recognize what he wants from you, and quickly respond to it. Unlike the culture around you, always dragging you down to its level of immaturity, God brings the best out of you, develops well-formed maturity in you."

We have to learn and retain the Word of God in our hearts as the Bible tells us in,

Romans 1:18-28 NIV *"The wrath of God is being revealed from heaven against all the godlessness and wickedness of people, who suppress the truth by their wickedness, 19 since what may be known about God is plain to them because God has made it plain to them. 20 For since the creation of the world God's invisible qualities his eternal power and divine nature have been seen, being understood from what has been made, so that people are without excuse. 21 For although they knew God, they neither glorified him as God nor gave thanks to him, but their thinking became futile, and their foolish hearts were darkened. 22 <u>Although they claimed to be wise, they became fools 23 and exchanged the glory of the immortal God for images made to look like a mortal human being and birds and animals and reptiles. 24 Therefore God gave them over in the sinful desires of their hearts to sexual impurity for the degrading of their bodies with one another. 25 They exchanged the truth about God for a lie, and worshiped and served created things rather than the Creator who is forever praised. Amen. 26 Because of this, God gave them over to shameful lusts. Even their women exchanged natural sexual relations for unnatural ones. 27 In the same way, the men also abandoned natural relations with women and were inflamed with lust for one another. Men committed shameful acts with other men and received in themselves the due penalty for their error. 28 Furthermore, just as they did not think it worthwhile to retain the knowledge of God, so God</u>*

The Dangers Of Not Renewing Your Mind

gave them over to a depraved mind so that they do what ought not to be done."

How does that scripture affect you? To think that it's possible to be given over to a depraved (perverted) mind; that you believe a lie, and don't realize that you are believing a lie, that's dangerous. We can't expect God to ignore our sinful ways when He has given us every opportunity to change. God spells out how He feels about us not giving His Word our utmost attention. I want to remind you of Ephesians 4:17-19, I shared in Chapter 3; "Taking Off The Old Man."

We hurt others as well as ourselves when we refuse to conform to the image of Christ. There are people relying on us to walk into our destiny. What we do now with the knowledge of God's Word will affect our family line for years to come, which can be good or bad. We will be a stepping stone to their growth with the knowledge that we learn and pass on, or we will be a stumbling block because we learned nothing to pass on. For example, you might be the first person in your family line that's born again, and if that's the case, God wants you to make sure that your family; your children, and your children's children, inherit salvation also. If you get saved and don't renew your mind to understand how valuable you are to God in bringing about His purpose in your life, you can forfeit your family line's salvation by not being about God's business. Can your children see Christ in you? Do you have a desire to teach them about Jesus and all that He has provided for them as His heirs? In some cases, if not all, God is starting a new way through you. Your family line will be better because you are saved, or they will continue down the same dark path of sin and destruction because you didn't renew your mind. We will stand before God when we leave this earth and give an account of our lives.

The Dangers Of Not Renewing Your Mind

I realize that this information may be a bit much to internalize, but it is necessary. We all can see the condition of our world, everyone doing their own thing, even Christians. When are we going to be God-fearing children of God who wants to please Him? God-fearing means that we reverence God. Reverence means a feeling or attitude of deep respect tinged with awe. It means, the outward manifestation of this feeling: to pay reverence, bow or curtsey.

I simply want to usher you into an amazing life in Christ. God wants your hearts. He wants to know that you have "a want to" in your heart to change and live for Him. Whether or not you are successful at conforming completely is not the question. Do you love Him enough to want what He wants?

There is a quote that says, *"preach the gospel and if necessary use words."* This means exactly what it says. Your actions speak louder than words. That is why non-believers label Christians hypocrites. We say one thing with our mouth and display something totally different with our actions. Another quote is, *"we are the only Jesus that some people will ever see."* As I mentioned before, we all won't preach from a church pulpit, but our lives are always preaching something. What are you preaching with your behavior in your sphere of influence? What about your co-workers? Do they see Jesus when they see you or are you a hypocrite to them? Are you one way at work and another person with a mask on at church? We must be the best Christians that we can be. Once our new walk begins, we have to protect what we learn.

2 Corinthians 3:2-3 (NKJV) *"You are our epistle written in our hearts, known and read by all men;* [3] *clearly you are an epistle of Christ, ministered by us, written not with ink but by the Spirit of the living God, not on tablets of stone but on tablets of flesh, that is, of the heart."*

The Dangers Of Not Renewing Your Mind

Here Paul is saying that as Christians, the Word that we learn and apply is being seen, thus making us the Epistles (letters to the world). We have the responsibility of representing our God and Father in a worthy manner. As I explained, the opposite is also true; let's not be a poor witness.

Proverbs 4:23 NIV states, *"Above all else, guard your heart, for it is the wellspring of life."*

The "heart" includes our mind. As our minds are being renewed, we have to guard or protect all of our gates; the eye gates, the ear gates, and what we speak out of our mouths. If you acknowledge that statement, it will affect the way you entertain yourself, as was previously stated. We can't allow anything or anyone to keep us from growing and walking into what God has called us to do. This is another quote from Apostle Mike Freeman, *"Get away from those who have your problem and get around those who have your answer."*

1 Corinthians 15:33 AMP *"Do not be deceived, bad company corrupts good character."*

Amos 3:3 TLB *"For how can we walk together with your sins between us?"* These scriptures speak for themselves and need no commentary. It's imperative that we surround ourselves with people that are going in the same direction as we are.

Proverbs 27:17 NKJV *As iron sharpens iron so a man sharpens the countenance of his friend.*

Another potential problem that can arise when you don't renew your mind is that you will not have confidence towards God.

The Dangers Of Not Renewing Your Mind

1 John 3:21 AMP *"And, beloved, if our consciences (our hearts) do not accuse us [if they do not make us feel guilty and condemn us], we have confidence (complete assurance and boldness) before God,"*

Having confidence in God is vital when praying and seeking Him. Being sensitive to His Holy Spirit when we have sinned will help in that area.

Matthew 5:23-24 *"if you are offering your gift at the altar and there remember that your brother or sister has something against you, 24 leave your gift there in front of the altar. First, go and be reconciled to them; then come and offer your gift."*

Repenting is a good habit to have. It assures us that our heart stays pure before God and if we do hurt someone, it's good to let them witness how a true Christian behaves when we are at fault. There have been times when I would repent to someone, and the person had no idea what I was talking about. In those times, it's just good to clear your conscience because it can affect your confidence in God, especially if the enemy jumps on board with it. What do I mean about the enemy jumping on board? The Bible tells us that he is standing before God accusing us day and night. **(Revelations 12:10)** The devil was kicked out of heaven so he can't accuse us to God, but he can and does accuse us to ourselves, condemning us for our mistakes. That is the enemy's Modus operandi (or M.O.). He wants to condemn us and cause us to focus on the mistake in hopes that we abort what God is doing in our lives. If he is able to overtake us in our thought life, we will miss some very important moments in our walk with God. We will make mistakes but don't let the mistakes overtake you.

The Dangers Of Not Renewing Your Mind

Romans 8:1 *"There is therefore now no condemnation to those who are in Christ Jesus, who do not walk according to the flesh, but according to the Spirit."*

I had a situation when I was working at the dental office. I had to adjust a partial denture, and while I was adjusting it, it slipped out of my hand and fell on the floor and broke. I was terrified! Fear overtook me. I repaired it and played it off like it had not happened. No one could tell that I had repaired it but I knew that was deception. I don't know why I thought I could just repent and be done with it? Holy Spirit nudged me and I had to do the right thing. Over the weekend I had no peace and I was very embarrassed over what I had done. I called my Doctor to tell him, of course he was understanding about the situation, and probably got a good laugh. I know that if I had ignored God's rebuke, I would have been ashamed before God in prayer. I repented to clear my conscious so that I could go before my Father with confidence. From that lesson, I learned that I will acknowledge what I've done immediately so that I don't have to deal with guilt. We are human and we will make mistakes; own them, repent and keep it moving. So I say the same thing to you, receive and walk in the forgiveness that Jesus died for you to have.

2 Corinthians 2:9-11 MSG *"Another reason I wrote you was to see if you would stand the test and be obedient to everything. 10 Anyone you forgive, I also forgive. And what I have forgiven if there was anything to forgive I have forgiven in the sight of Christ for your sake, in order that Satan might not outwit us. For we are not unaware of his schemes."*

There will be a conviction on the inside when something is wrong. Investigate that conviction and ask God to reveal what it is if it's not obvious. It does not mean that you are in trouble with God, but it does mean that He's getting your attention

The Dangers Of Not Renewing Your Mind

regarding something that you are oblivious to and understand that it's a teachable moment. He wants to make sure that you are aware of any behavior that's not appropriate so that you don't continue to make the same mistakes. I spoke of those nudges. He is our Father, and He must correct us as any good parent would. Look at these verses in Hebrews from the Message Bible:

Hebrews 12:5-12 MSG *"My dear child, don't shrug off God's discipline, but don't be crushed by it either. It's the child he loves that he disciplines; the child he embraces, he also corrects. God is educating you; that's why you must never drop out. He's treating you as dear children. This trouble you're in isn't punishment; it's training, the normal experience of children. Only irresponsible parents leave children to fend for themselves. Would you prefer an irresponsible God? We respect our own parents for training and not spoiling us, so why not embrace God's training so we can truly live? While we were children, our parents did what seemed best to them. But God is doing what is best for us, training us to live God's holy best. At the time, discipline isn't much fun. It always feels like it's going against the grain. Later, of course, it pays off handsomely, for it's the well-trained who find themselves mature in their relationship with God."*

I absolutely love, love, love the scriptures. They give us so much hope when we are confident that God is for us and not against us. One thing is for sure, as long as we are in these bodies, we will make mistakes, but we can run to God with those mistakes and not away from Him in shame. It is so important to have a pure heart. To have a pure heart means you have no hidden agendas or motive; being transparent and a desire to please God. People with a pure heart don't feel the need to wear a mask; they will not be labeled a hypocrite. Having a pure heart will keep you healthy spiritually, and that

The Dangers Of Not Renewing Your Mind

is very important also. I share these stories from my own experience because I try not to go through anything without learning something from it. Apostle Mike taught us that "Sometimes we win and sometimes we learn; if we learn we never lose." That was so profound to me, and I understood it completely from my own life lessons. My spiritual process has been interesting because I am very hard on myself. Although I knew that God loved me and His grace was available to me, I didn't receive it as I should have. Instead I beat myself up over the mistakes I made. The enemy didn't have to condemn me because I condemned myself. I realized later that I was so preoccupied stewing over my mistakes that I was missing what I was to gain from the situation. I wasn't learning anything, and if I had continued in that cycle, I would have missed the lesson and continued down the path of "woe is me," remaining ignorant, and having not grown in that particular area of my life. Trust me when I say, our sin or mistakes don't take God by surprise. He already knows.

In those times when we've "missed it," we have to acknowledge the conviction of Holy Spirit and repent but, ignore the condemnation of the enemy because we are forgiven. I told you to just ignore him, but we can't ignore him. The enemy is Sabbath-less (never rests) and will not give up in trying to destroy us if there is a place that he can lay claim to in our lives.

Ephesians 4:27 AMP *"Leave no [such] room or foothold for the devil [give no opportunity to him]."*

He is ruthless, and we have to be also. We must combat his suggestions and lies with the Word of God. Tell him "it is written" and then we must declare out of our mouths who we are in Christ and say what God has said about us. Now, if we don't know what God has done for us and what He has said about us, we will not get the victory over the enemy in our

The Dangers Of Not Renewing Your Mind

lives. As I said, he is ruthless and wants to destroy us. It's time-out for letting the devil have control over our lives when he is supposed to be under our feet. The scripture tells us that, "The same power that raised Jesus from the dead resides on the inside of us.

Romans 8:11-13 AMP *"And if the Spirit of Him Who raised up Jesus from the dead dwells in you, [then] He Who raised up Christ Jesus from the dead will also restore to life your mortal (short-lived, perishable) bodies through His Spirit Who dwells in you. 12 So then, brethren, we are debtors, but not to the flesh [we are not obligated to our carnal nature], to live [a life ruled by the standards set up by the dictates] of the flesh. 13 For if you live according to [the dictates of] the flesh, you will surely die. But if through the power of the [Holy] Spirit you are [habitually] putting to death [making extinct, deadening] the [evil] deeds prompted by the body, you shall [really and genuinely] live forever."*

We have to ask ourselves, what are we doing with all of that power? We can't continue to waste the grace that is existing on the inside of us. We must renew our minds!!

Galatians 2:21 NIV *"I do not set aside the grace of God, for if righteousness could be gained through the law Christ died for nothing!"*

So how are we frustrating the grace of God? This is a question that we need to explore so that we don't continue a cycle of not understanding what the Word is saying. We don't want to keep going around the same mountain and not going into the promise land. When trials surface in our lives, it's crucial to press into God because those are pivotal times to learn and gain understanding. He sent Jesus to help; Holy Spirit is standing by ready to assist us and give us the victory in all areas, but when we forget about Him, and handle our issues apart from His Spirit, we forfeit the grace that could be ours. That is how we frustrate the grace of God. We set God's help aside as if we don't need Him; thus making what He did for us, through Jesus in vain. God's amazing grace is available to us, so remember that when the tests come, be aware that He is there and invite Him into the situation. Our Father wants to be hands-on in our lives, but because we lack the understanding of His grace, we go through our difficult situations alone instead of going to God. Always seek His wisdom and how to overcome any situation. There is a lesson to be learned in every trial we face, so it's important to gain wisdom from it. Once we have wisdom in a situation, we can help others.

Gaining Wisdom

According to the Christian Bible Reference Site; Wisdom in the biblical sense is the "ability to judge correctly and to follow the best course of action, based on knowledge and understanding" (Lockyer p. 1103) We are instructed to gain wisdom.

Proverbs 19:8 AMP *"He who gains wisdom and good sense loves (preserves) his own soul; He who keeps understanding will find good and prosper."*

Having said that, with life's trials, we are to strive for wisdom by understanding what we have gone through so that we are more knowledgeable. Wisdom is knowing how to apply good judgment and common sense to situations. God is our source of all wisdom and we can ask Him for it.

The Dangers Of Not Renewing Your Mind

James 1:5 KJV *"If any of you lacks wisdom, let him ask God, who gives generously to all without reproach, and it will be given him."*

Proverbs 4:7. *"Wisdom is the principal thing; therefore get wisdom and in all your getting get understanding."*

After we have gone through a trial, we've gained an experience with God, as well as wisdom, that we otherwise would not have gained if we had not gone through the trial. For instance, you may have a bill that needs to be paid, but you don't have the money, you pray about the situation and soon after that, you receive a check in the mail for the amount you need. In that trial, you experienced God as your provider. That might sound farfetched to you, but it happens all of the time for God's children. He is a multifaceted God; there is no end to His attributes. So in all your getting, get an understanding. I can't say this enough, always ask God what it is you are supposed to learn in the trial. God's motive in our trials is always to cause us to grow in wisdom. Nothing that we go through will be wasted as long as we get God on the scene. If we can keep our eyes on God, *"All things work together for good to those who love God, to those who are the called according to His purpose."* **(*Romans 8:28*)**
"All things" consist of good, bad, happy, sad and anything in between. Read the story of Joseph and learn why it is possible for all things to work together for good. It is inevitable that we will experience evil things, but it does not come from God. Most, if not all, of us have suffered some abusive treatment from people that have caused us to change the way we view people, life, and even God. But what happened to us was not the will of God. And it is for those horrible reasons that Jesus came to rescue us. When we invited Jesus into our lives, remember we gave Him all of that abuse and negativity, and what the enemy meant for bad, God can make something

The Dangers Of Not Renewing Your Mind

beautiful out of it. We've all heard the sayings; God can take our mess and make it our message or take the test and make it our testimony. When the tests come, we can be thankful that we don't have to go through any situation alone. He is ever present to help us. If we submit to the whole plan of God, He will take our devastation and cause it to benefit others, using us as an instrument for the kingdom.

I remember the story of Joseph from *Genesis 37* and all of the abuse he suffered at the hands of his brothers. His father favored Joseph more than he favored his older brothers, and they hated him for that. Joseph had a dream and told his brothers about the dream, and the content of the dream made them hate him even more. I will make a long story short. One day Joseph's brothers went to feed the flock, and his father sent him to see if his brothers were ok. Before Joseph could reach his brothers, they saw him coming, and they conspired to kill him. Reuben, one of his brothers, would not allow the others to kill him. He had a plan of his own to save Joseph's life and bring him back home to their father, but there was a caravan passing by and the other brothers sold Joseph to the Ishmaelite's. They returned home without Joseph and told their father that he was killed by an animal. Please go and read the entire account of this story. It is a remarkable account of Joseph's faith in his God. Picking the story back up in chapter 45, we see that the tables are turned, and Joseph's dream is coming to pass. Unbeknownst to his brothers, Joseph ended up being second in charge of Pharaoh's kingdom, and he was running things. The brothers had no idea that they would ever see Joseph again but look at what Joseph said to his brothers when they were reunited.

Genesis 45:5-8 NET *"Now, do not be upset and do not be angry with yourselves because you sold me here, for God sent me ahead of you to preserve life! For these past two years* *there has been famine in the land, and for five more years there will be neither plowing nor harvesting. God sent me ahead of you to preserve you on the earth and to save your lives by a great deliverance. So now, it is not you who sent me here, but God. He has made me an adviser to Pharaoh, lord over all his household, and ruler over all the land of Egypt."*

Genesis 50:20 *"As for you, you meant to harm me, but God intended it for a good purpose, so he could preserve the lives of many people, as you can see this day."*

Oh My Goodness!! What a story!! What would the Kingdom of God be like if every single one of His children processed their trials the way Joseph did? He suffered many things at the hands of many people but he was matured in his thinking, and God used him mightily. That's a real faith walk.

"He endured hardship as a good soldier" **(2 Timothy 2:3)** just as the scripture instructs us to. This verse reminds me of a renowned Bible teacher and author, who was raped by her father for many years. She could not believe that God allowed her to go through that but after she submitted to the Lordship of Jesus Christ, He delivered her from the hurt and shame she suffered, and she was able to forgive her father. She ministered to him to receive Jesus as his Lord and Savior, baptized him in water, and took care of him until he died. What a testimony! This is the kind of testimonies we can have when we progress in renewing our mind. Just like Joseph, she ministered to her abuser and God restored him. But look closely at this because God was not only interested in the one who suffered the abuse but the abuser also. How does that make you feel to know that God loves the abuser and wants them to know Him also. She denied herself the privilege of hating her father; instead, she was obedient to God when He told her it was time to confront him. She had no idea what

The Dangers Of Not Renewing Your Mind

God was doing at that time, but she submitted. When she was suffering abuse at the hand of her father, she had no idea that she would one day be a renowned world Bible teacher and author, ministering to hurting people all over the world. God turned it around in her life.

Psalms 30:11-12 NKJV *"You have turned for me my mourning into dancing; You have put off my sackcloth and clothed me with gladness, 12 To the end that my glory may sing praise to You and not be silent. O LORD my God, I will give thanks to You forever."*

That is what God wants to do for every one of us. He wants to turn our mourning into dancing, turn our sorrow into joy, give us beauty for ashes, but we have to want Him to do it. If He allows the trial, He can use it for His glory. This is why it is so important to renew our minds to His ways. It is vital that we *"study to show ourselves approved, a workman that need not be ashamed, rightly dividing the Word of truth,"* **(2 Timothy 2:15)** so that we can experience all the freedom that is ours in Christ. Our freedom is in Jesus Christ, but we have to study and renew our minds in His Word. No one can do that for us. There is one more scripture that I need to share that's very important to know.

Ephesians 4:30 MSG *"Don't grieve God. Don't break his heart. His Holy Spirit, moving and breathing in you, is the most intimate part of your life, making you fit for Himself. Don't take such a gift for granted."*

Once again, we see that when we ignore what God has done for us we grieve Him. Please don't take His gifts for granted. He has done everything possible for us to succeed in our new lifestyle. Become a vessel that is fit for His purpose so that He can get the glory from our lives.

The Dangers Of Not Renewing Your Mind

So, I started this chapter by telling you the danger of not renewing your mind. I pray that I have shed some insight. We need God on our side, and He is on our side, but we can't be ignorant of His Word. The enemy is banking on us being ignorant and void of understanding. The Word tells us in

Hosea 4:6 *"My people are destroyed for lack of knowledge."*

What you don't know can hurt you. It is vital to not only understand the Kingdom of God (God's way of doing and being right) but to know how the enemy operates also. He is always looking for an open door in our lives so that he can take advantage of us.

1 Peter 5:8 NKJV *"Be sober, be vigilant; because your adversary the devil walks about like a roaring lion, seeking whom he may devour."*

Don't worry about what the enemy is trying to do in your life if you are diligently seeking God because the weapon will be formed, but the Word tells us that it will not prosper, and that is what our focus must be on; "it will not prosper." We have to watch and pray.

2 Corinthians 2:11 MSG says, *"After all, we don't want to unwittingly give Satan an opening for yet more mischief we're not oblivious to his sly ways!"*

We have to settle in our minds that we are lifetime learners in the ways of God. The world is not going to hand us anything that pertains to God so we must go after it. The devil is real, and he also has a plan for our life. In fact, he's been working his plan in our lives all of our lives as unbelievers, and he will continue working his plan even when we become believers.

The Dangers Of Not Renewing Your Mind

But if we are God's children, we are no longer subject to him, but he's not going to leave us alone just because we are Christians. Let me remind you of his motive as the thief and the accuser. He wants to steal, kill, and destroy you and your purpose. But, the only power he has over you is the power you give him.

Luke 10:19 AMP *"Listen carefully: I have given you authority [that you now possess] to tread on serpents and scorpions, and [the ability to exercise authority] over all the power of the enemy (Satan); and nothing will [in any way] harm you."*

This scripture will mean something to those who will learn who they are in God. The authority you have been given is **power**. Do not say yes to your adoption and God's redeeming grace and never renew your mind from your old ways of doing life when He has given you the power to resist sin. Our destiny in God depends on us walking upright before Him.

1 John 1:7 *NIV "But if we walk in the light, as he is in the light, we have fellowship with one another, and the blood of Jesus, his Son, purifies us from all sin."*

John 4:23-24 *NKJV "But the hour is coming, and now is, when the true worshipers will worship the Father in spirit and truth; for the Father is seeking such to worship Him. God is Spirit, and those who worship Him must worship in Spirit and truth."*

We must exercise self-control (one of the nine fruits of the Spirit). We can't run the risk of forfeiting our inheritance as God's children. I cannot stress enough that God has an established system in place through Jesus the Christ, full of grace and power, to accomplish His purpose in our lives. we

The Dangers Of Not Renewing Your Mind

cannot bypass His system to do it our way and expect His stamp of approval on it. Our good deeds will not satisfy God or influence Him to give us anything, including heaven. You will be gravely disappointed.

What I didn't realize until I trusted God, was that the very things I wanted to hold on to were the very things the enemy was using to destroy me. We all know from experience that sin is pleasurable, but in some cases, it ends up destroying us because it becomes an addiction that we can't break on our own. There is a saying that "*Sin will take you where you don't want to go and keep you there longer than you want to stay.*" No one grows up desiring to be in bondage, but it happens to all of us in some kind of way. I know for myself that God is a delivering God.

As I am writing, I'm being reminded of the time when I smoked, and I tried to quit. I was not able to break the habit on my own. After I received Jesus, I continued in my old nature for about two weeks before I had a conversation with God about drinking and smoking. I said to the Lord, "If You don't want me to drink and smoke, please take the taste for the alcohol and cigarettes out of my mouth because I enjoy it." I prayed that prayer and did not really expect anything to happen because I didn't know He was that personal. On a Friday evening, one of my mentors invited me to Bible study, but I was still in the old way of thinking. I declined her invitation because it was Friday and I always partied or just relaxed on Friday. However, when I decided to sit in front of the TV with my wine and cigarettes, the taste for both was gone. The cigarettes were horrible, and I didn't desire the wine. From that day to this one, I have never desired either, and that was almost 30 years ago. And there were no withdrawal symptoms. To God be the glory!!! I honestly believe God did that for me so that I could know that He is real and that He is aware and interested in the progression of my life in His Kingdom. I believe He does that for all of His children so that we can experience His goodness in a personal way. In that initial act, I knew Him as a deliverer. I believe that is part of the miracle of the new birth. He wants us to experience Him and know Him, and be fully persuaded in our hearts that we can trust Him to work His plan through us.

Ephesians 3:20 NKJV *"Now to Him who is able to do exceedingly abundantly above all that we ask or think, according to the power that works in us,"*

Whatever God put us on this earth to do He promised to do it through us. Two of my favorite scriptures are:

Philippians 4:13 NKJV *"I can do all things through Christ who strengthens me."*

This scripture is saying that whatever our assignments are, not every assignment in the world, but only our assignments, we can accomplish it in Jesus' strength. So when we discover why we are here, we don't have to wonder if we can accomplish it or not. Yes, some assignments will be challenging, but even in that, God will cause us to triumph if we don't quit, give up on Him, or lose heart in the process. Our assignments are designed to give God glory and bring much pleasure to us as well.

Proverbs 16:3 AMP *"Roll your works upon the Lord [commit and trust them wholly to Him; He will cause your thoughts to become agreeable to His will, and] so shall your plans be established and succeed."*

It doesn't get any better than that. God is interested in our success, and He is working with us to make it happen. All we must do is put our trust in Him, meditate on His Word and

The Dangers Of Not Renewing Your Mind

watch it come to pass. Dr. Dee Dee Freeman teaches that we must focus on the promise and not the process. I am still learning to keep my eyes on the promise because the process can look bleak. But as long as I keep my eyes on God, I can view any problem as a part of my growth process. As I mentioned before, His perspective is better than mine. Life is full of tests, and we will never know how we have grown without them. Much of what I have shared in this chapter carries over to partnering with God in chapter six.

Partnering With God

Let me start by saying, God never meant for us to live independently of Him. He has employed us to work with Him. What an honor it is to be hired by The Almighty God, who has become everything we will ever need in our lives. He wants to show off through us.

1 Corinthians 3:9 NIV *"For we are co-workers in God's service; you are God's field, God's building."*

2 Corinthians 6:1 NIV *"As God's co-workers we urge you not to receive God's grace in vain."*

Remember we talked about grace being God's ability working in our lives. In my former life, I couldn't have imagined God wanting to recruit me as His Partner. But that is exactly what the scripture tells us. So why has God chosen us to collaborate with Him?

2 Corinthians 5:20 NKJV says *"Now then, we are ambassadors for Christ, as though God were pleading through us: we implore you on Christ's behalf, be reconciled to God.* In verse 18 it says, *"We have the ministry of reconciliation."*

God has called the born-again Christian to operate on His behalf. We are the mouthpiece for Him on the earth as stated in a previous chapter. I mentioned this before, but it bears repeating;

Romans 10:14 NKJV *"How then shall they call on Him in whom they have not believed? And how shall they believe in*

Him of whom they have not heard? And how shall they hear without a preacher?"

God has put a system in place to redeem mankind back to Himself, and He invites us to partner with Him in doing so. He operates from a different system than we do and if we want to obtain God's best, it will have to be on Kingdom terms (His way of doing things). I've said all of that before but we can't hear it enough. Look at this next scripture and think about if you or any of the people you know operate like God.

Matthew 5:43-45 gives us a glimpse of God's system. *"You have heard that it was said, 'You shall love your neighbor and hate your enemy.' But I say to you, love your enemies, bless those who curse you, do good to those who hate you, and pray for those who spitefully use you and persecute you, that you may be sons of your Father in heaven; for He makes His sun rise on the evil and on the good, and sends rain on the just and on the unjust."*

How many people do you know will automatically bless those who curse them? I know Christians that have grown in that manner but they didn't start off that way. Growing continually in the ways of God is what separates sons from the children. Not everyone grows up in God to be a "son"; used of Him to satisfy His agenda. Babies never see the big picture, all they focus on is what they want and never comprehend that they are here on this earth to be used of God. I emphasize "son" because it connotes maturity. Let's take a look at some examples from the scriptures of those who cooperated with the plan of God whether they understood the whole picture or not. Joseph comes to mind again, but I've already explained how Joseph responded to God's purpose for His life. So let us look at the account of Daniel and his three Hebrew friends. They were four faithful young prophets of God who were taken captive by King Nebuchadnezzar. In their captivity, Daniel gained favor with the king when he gave the king the interpretation of a dream, and he was promoted to Chief Governor over the king's province. To make this long story very short, there were two commissioners that were envious of Daniel and wanted to see him fall. They took note that Daniel had an "excellent spirit" and knew that no one would find any fault with him. So they tricked the king by having him sign a decree that anyone who prayed to another God other than the king for thirty days would be put in the lion's den. They knew that Daniel prayed to his God. Well, they knew he was praying, and they told the king, and the king was displeased with himself because of the decree he'd made. He really liked Daniel but he had to go through with what he had decreed, but even the king knew that Daniel's God was the true and living God, and he told Daniel, your God will deliver you. The Bible says that the king spent the night fasting for Daniel and he didn't sleep at all that night.

Daniel 6:19-22 NKJV *"Then the king arose very early in the morning and went in haste to the den of lions. And when he came to the den, he cried out with a lamenting voice to Daniel. The king spoke, saying to Daniel, "Daniel, servant of the living God, has your God, whom you serve continually, been able to deliver you from the lions?" 21 Then Daniel said to the king, "O king, live forever! 22 My God sent His angel and shut the lions' mouths so that they have not hurt me because I was found innocent before Him; and also, O king, I have done no wrong before you."*

What an awesome account of Daniel's faithfulness to God and the awesomeness of our God to protect him. Now let's look at Daniel's three friends that were just as faithful to God as he was. Their names are Shadrach, Meshach, and Abed-Nego. Another long story short, these guys refused to fall down and worship the golden image that King Nebuchadnezzar set up. The consequence of their action was to be thrown into the fiery furnace, but they didn't deviate from their faith in God to deliver them. Let's read their response.

Daniel 3:16-18 NKJV *Shadrach, Meshach, and Abed-Nego answered and said to the king, "O Nebuchadnezzar, we have no need to answer you in this matter. 17 If that is the case, our God whom we serve is able to deliver us from the burning fiery furnace, and He will deliver us from your hand, O king. 18 But if not, let it be known to you, O king, that we do not serve your gods, nor will we worship the gold image which you have set up."*

What was my reason for sharing these stories? These were accounts of those who operated as mature believers to their God. They were firm in their stance not to compromise what they believed even in the face of being thrown into the lion's den and the fiery furnace. In their stance to worship only God, God's faithfulness to them was demonstrated loud and clear throughout Nebuchadnezzar's kingdom. I'm thankful for their testimony, and the testament of God's faithfulness to them, and to us now, as His children. If He did it for them, He would do it for us. He wants to see us operating in the gifts and callings that He blessed us with, but it's unfortunate that many people never come into the understanding of why they are here or grow to maturity in their walk with the Lord. So understand that as God's children, He has employed us to the nations to share of His goodness.

Matthew 28:18-19 NKJV *And Jesus came and spoke to them, saying, "All authority has been given to Me in heaven and on earth. 19 Go therefore and make disciples of all the nations, baptizing them in the name of the Father and of the Son and of the Holy Spirit,"*

Partnering With God

My final quote from Apostle Mike Freeman is, "God's last commandment should be our first priority." As I quoted before, "We must make the Great Commission our main mission" in life because that is the work God put us here to do. We can be confident that God will help us as we are obedient to Him.

Philippians 2:13 NKJV *"for it is God who works in you both to will and to do for His good pleasure."*

God will work His plan through us if we let Him. When we take to heart what God wants, He promises us that He will make it happen. As I shared before, *Proverbs 16:3* is one of my favorite scriptures. I use it often to encourage myself that if what I'm doing is in the will of God my efforts will succeed.

Proverbs 16:3 AMPC *"Roll your works upon the Lord [commit and trust them wholly to Him; He will cause your thoughts to become agreeable to His will, and] so shall your plans be established and succeed."*

People are God's greatest treasure, and we must value souls the way God values souls. If we are truly operating in God's love and accomplishing His will, we'll share the Good News of the Gospel with those around us. Our efforts will not be in vain. You might be the one who plants the seed of the Word, someone else will water the seed, (Word) but please understand and believe that God will cause that seed to grow in the life of that person we shared it with. *(1 Corinthians 3:6)* In that process, you would have done your part to accomplish the will of the Father. He depends on you. Will you answer the call?

Conclusion

In conclusion, I want to stress the love that God has for all humanity. There is so much more to share about all that was discussed in this book. I only scratched the surface. He created us to be in fellowship with Him from the foundation of the world. He wants our worship, our love, and our fellowship. So that is why it is so important to find a good bible based teaching church to support you on your journey.

Although the fellowship was broken through no fault of our own, it is our responsibility to accept the invitation (salvation plan) that is offered to us through His Son, Jesus. Make your adoption sure. It is not His will for any of us to spend eternity separated from Him. Jesus is our only way back to God, and with accepting His provision, we have been given everything we need to live a holy, faith-filled life. We have to be active participants in our renewed lives. The benefits are endless with God. And while we are growing from faith to faith, we are to bring as many people that we can into a relationship with Jesus. If we love God and want to please Him, let us do what He put us on this earth to do. This is a great work that takes time, but it is a doable work if we allow God to do it through us. You may not know where to start. You can start by giving God your attention. Pray to Him out of a sincere heart, and He will answer. Refer back to Faith and Grace in chapter 3 and remember that you can trust Him to help you along.

Jeremiah 33:3 (NKJV) *"Call to Me, and I will answer you, and show you great and mighty things, which you do not know."*

God did not intend for us to come into the world and not know why we are here. I pray I have convinced you from scriptures in the Holy Bible to live a life pleasing to our Heavenly Father. God is intentional and you being here is no mistake. God brought you here for a divine purpose. Fulfill that purpose so that your life here on earth is not in vain as it relates to God's Kingdom. Our goal is to hear, *"Well done my good and faithful servant."* Here are a few more scriptures that I would like to leave with you.

I believe 1 & 2 Thessalonians can sum up this book.

1 Thessalonians 4:1-17 (NIV)

Living to Please God
4 "As for other matters, brothers and sisters, we instructed you how to live in order to please God, as in fact you are living. Now we ask you and urge you in the Lord Jesus to do this more and more. ² For you know what instructions we gave you by the authority of the Lord Jesus.
³ It is God's will that you should be sanctified: that you should avoid sexual immorality; ⁴ that each of you should learn to control your own body in a way that is holy and honorable, ⁵ not in passionate lust like the pagans, who do not know God; ⁶ and that in this matter no one should wrong or take advantage of a brother or sister. The Lord will punish all those who commit such sins, as we told you and warned you before. ⁷ For God did not call us to be impure, but to live a holy life. ⁸ Therefore, anyone who rejects this instruction does not reject a human being but God, the very God who gives you his Holy Spirit. ⁹ Now about your love for one another we do not need to write to you, for you yourselves have been taught by God to love each other.¹⁰ And in fact, you do love all of God's family throughout Macedonia. Yet we urge you, brothers and sisters, to do so more and more,¹¹ and to make it

your ambition to lead a quiet life: You should mind your own business and work with your hands, just as we told you, [12] so that your daily life may win the respect of outsiders and so that you will not be dependent on anybody.

Believers Who Have Died

[13] Brothers and sisters, we do not want you to be uninformed about those who sleep in death, so that you do not grieve like the rest of mankind, who have no hope. [14] For we believe that Jesus died and rose again and so we believe that God will bring with Jesus those who have fallen asleep in him. [15] According to the Lord's word, we tell you that we who are still alive, who are left until the coming of the Lord, will certainly not precede those who have fallen asleep. [16] For the Lord himself will come down from heaven, with a loud command, with the voice of the archangel and with the trumpet call of God, and the dead in Christ will rise first. [17] After that, we who are still alive and are left will be caught up together with them in the clouds to meet the Lord in the air. And so we will be with the Lord forever.

1 Thessalonians 5:1-25 (NIV)
The Day of the Lord

5 Now, brothers and sisters, about times and dates we do not need to write to you, [2] for you know very well that the day of the Lord will come like a thief in the night. [3] While people are saying, "Peace and safety," destruction will come on them suddenly, as labor pains on a pregnant woman, and they will not escape.
[4] But you, brothers and sisters, are not in darkness so that this day should surprise you like a thief. [5] You are all children of the light and children of the day. We do not belong to the night or to the darkness. [6] So then, let us not be like others, who are asleep, but let us be awake and sober. [7] For those who sleep, sleep at night, and those who get drunk, get drunk at

night. *⁸* But since we belong to the day, let us be sober, putting on faith and love as a breastplate, and the hope of salvation as a helmet. *⁹* For God did not appoint us to suffer wrath but to receive salvation through our Lord Jesus Christ. *¹⁰* He died for us so that, whether we are awake (living) or asleep (dead), we may live together with him. *¹¹* Therefore encourage one another and build each other up, just as in fact you are doing.

Final Instructions

¹² Now we ask you, brothers and sisters, to acknowledge those who work hard among you, who care for you in the Lord and who admonish you. *¹³* Hold them in the highest regard in love because of their work. Live in peace with each other. *¹⁴* And we urge you, brothers and sisters, warn those who are idle and disruptive, encourage the disheartened, help the weak, be patient with everyone. *¹⁵* Make sure that nobody pays back wrong for wrong, but always strive to do what is good for each other and for everyone else.
¹⁶ Rejoice always, *¹⁷* pray continually, *¹⁸* give thanks in all circumstances; for this is God's will for you in Christ Jesus.
¹⁹ Do not quench the Spirit. *²⁰* Do not treat prophecies with contempt *²¹* but test them all; hold on to what is good, *²²* reject every kind of evil.
²³ May God himself, the God of peace, sanctify you through and through. May your whole spirit, soul and body be kept blameless at the coming of our Lord Jesus Christ. *²⁴* The one who calls you is faithful, and he will do it.
²⁵ Brothers and sisters, pray for us.

2 Thessalonians 2:1-16(NIV)
The Man of Lawlessness

2 Concerning the coming of our Lord Jesus Christ and our being gathered to him, we ask you, brothers and sisters, *²* not to become easily unsettled or alarmed by the teaching allegedly from us whether by a prophecy or by word of mouth

or by letter asserting that the day of the Lord has already come. ³ Don't let anyone deceive you in any way, for that day will not come until the rebellion occurs and the man of lawlessness is revealed, the man doomed to destruction. ⁴ He will oppose and will exalt himself over everything that is called God or is worshiped, so that he sets himself up in God's temple, proclaiming himself to be God.

⁵ Don't you remember that when I was with you I used to tell you these things? ⁶ And now you know what is holding him back, so that he may be revealed at the proper time. ⁷ For the secret power of lawlessness is already at work; but the one who now holds it back will continue to do so till he is taken out of the way. ⁸ And then the lawless one will be revealed whom the Lord Jesus will overthrow with the breath of his mouth and destroy by the splendor of his coming. ⁹ The coming of the lawless one will be in accordance with how Satan works. He will use all sorts of displays of power through signs and wonders that serve the lie, ¹⁰ and all the ways that wickedness deceives those who are perishing. They perish because they refused to love the truth and so be saved. ¹¹ For this reason God sends them a powerful delusion so that they will believe the lie¹² and so that all will be condemned who have not believed the truth but have delighted in wickedness.

Stand Firm

¹³ But we ought always to thank God for you, brothers and sisters loved by the Lord, because God chose you as first fruits to be saved through the sanctifying work of the Spirit and through belief in the truth. ¹⁴ He called you to this through our gospel that you might share in the glory of our Lord Jesus Christ.

¹⁵ So then, brothers and sisters, stand firm and hold fast to the teachings we passed on to you, whether by word of mouth or by letter.

¹⁶ May our Lord Jesus Christ himself and God our Father, who loved us and by his grace gave us eternal encouragement and good hope, encourage your hearts and strong.

Final Greetings
2 Thessalonians 3:16-18 (NIV)
¹⁶ Now may the Lord of peace himself give you peace at all times and in every way. The Lord be with all of you.
¹⁷ I, Paul, write this greeting in my own hand, which is the distinguishing mark in all my letters. This is how I write.
¹⁸ The grace of our Lord Jesus Christ be with you all."

REFERENCES
Dictionary.com
Quotes from Apostle Michael A. Freeman; Spirit of Faith Christian Center (SOFCC)
Quote from Dr. Deloris Freeman; Spirit of Faith Christian Center (SOFCC)
Song Lyrics Courtesy of AZLyrics.

About The Author

April C. Pryde, affectionately known as Tia, is a wife, mother, grandmother, minister, entrepreneur, and an author.

Her Christian Journey began when she received Jesus Christ as her Savior in 1989 at Mason Temple Church of God in Christ in Conway, SC and she has been serving the Lord in various capacities ever since.

As a babe in Christ and excited about God, she served in the ministry of helps doing whatever her hands found to do. She loved sharing the Word of God with her family and friends and desired to mentor God's women. As she grew in the Word, the Lord promoted her in every church she attended in their military travels. While serving at Word of Life Christian Center in Honolulu Hawaii, the Lord lead her to open the first home cell group on Hickam Air Force Base where for two years, she and her husband Bud facilitated a cell group bringing clarity to the Word of God.

After serving 5 1/2 years in Hawaii, they relocated to Japan, where she led the Women's Ministry and then on to Maryland, where she continued to lead the Women's Ministry for a time, encouraging women to develop a vibrant relationship with God and to discover their purpose.

She attended Spirit of Faith Bible Institute and received a diploma in Biblical Studies and is currently serving in various ministries under Apostle Mike and Dr. Deloris Freeman of Spirit of Faith Christian Center. She currently teaches a home bible study and continues to mentor women, family, and friends in the Word of God. She realizes that there is much to be done in the body of Christ and is excited about advancing the Kingdom of God and fulfilling her destiny.

www.ingramcontent.com/pod-product-compliance
Lightning Source LLC
Chambersburg PA
CBHW050435010526
44118CB00013B/1541